1-800-OH-MY-DONALD

OMD : Opinions of Mass Destruction

(of the status quo)

contemporary writs by

CHRIS BENT

www.chrisbent.com

Published in the USA by Chris Bent
Naples, Florida USA
http://ChrisBent.com

1-800-I-AM-UNHAPPY,
1-800-FOR-WOMEN-ONLY,
1-800-LAUGHING-OUT-LOUD,
1-800-OH-MY-GOODNESS,
1-800-FOR-SEALS-ONLY, and
1-800-OH-MY-DONALD
are trademarks owned by
Chris Bent and are used with his permission.

———◆•◆◆•◆———

Also By Chris Bent

Available in Paperback and Electronic Versions

1-800-I-AM-UNHAPPY
Volume 1

1-800-I-AM-UNHAPPY
Volume 2

1-800-FOR-WOMEN-ONLY

1-800-LAUGHING-OUT-LOUD

1-800-OH-MY-GOODNESS

1-800-FOR-SEALS-ONLY

Coming Soon:

1-800-FOR-VETERANS-ONLY

DEDICATION

To Christina, Candice, Courtney and their journeys . . .
and to Carlos and Vickie. . . .

Prologue

This is meant to be a book for just one person. If just that one person is touched in some way to make their journey better, then the effort is not in vain. Each one of us can look back to one moment that changed our direction for the better. May this book, a collection of my writs and wit, find that pair of eyes.

Chris Bent

Kennebunkport
September 2015
www.ChrisBent.com

Contents

Chapters

This book is not meant to be an endorsement of any candidate for the Presidency of the United States.

As I wrote this book the visions and strategies had yet to be detailed by any candidate. And, as we know, all plans are all subject to change and modification as circumstances evolve.

However, Mr. Donald Trump, like it or not, has forced discussion that would never have happened or that would have been neutered in endless talking points.

We the people want brains and heart. We all see our nation adrift and facing incredible evil forces from within and abroad.

The Donald is sure controversial, but who cares? We get to see someone willing to make mistakes and show some passion for his potential. We applaud. He has raised the bar. Now it is up to both parties to show their stuff.

The status quo is a no go.

Enjoy the book, I did.

1-800-OH-MY-DONALD

OMD: Opinions Of Mass Destruction

(Of the Status Quo)

inspirational writs by

CHRIS BENT

Note of Compilation

As this book was inspired by the rapid political changes this last year as a plethora of candidates vied for ranking. Unlike any other time. The vision was to be a book solely on politics and the future of your nation.

Since the first book 1-800-I-AM-UNHAPPY the theme of waste of lives, vision, and values was always present. To create this book I have drawn chapters from all my 6 books along with new Trump centered ones.

You might say this is an anthology of sorts.

Or just OMD, Opinions of Mass Destruction...... of the status quo.

It's the Hair

First things first.

It's about the hair.

Can't get beyond it.

How can such an interesting guy have such a distracting look?

John Lennon! The hair hung down almost over his eyes. The Beatles landed in New York City on Feb 7, 1964. Girls were screaming insanely. Hair has never been the same since.

Older people thought they looked absurd. The young couldn't stop their feet from dancing. They wanted to dance again…and differently.

After a while you got used to the hair. Ed Sullivan's greased head was sure a contrast. But the music was finally more important than the hair. To this day their harmony echoes in our heads. Not to be forgotten for generations. Peace and love and hair.

Sometimes we have to look beneath the surface to see what is going on. We have all sorts of investigations demanding that

everything is exposed. We demand the truth. Except that truth is found in how you live and whether your words are truths.

Shave the head and do you find out what it thinks?? Or strip one naked and do you know what one thinks?

Spontaneity is paramount. If someone just talks without prompters and talking points you can get a feel of who they are. It's not the hair.

Which politician has the best hair? Sometimes it helps on TV. But what they say and how they say it is more important. Are they one of us?

It's a great white baseball cap.

Good hair doesn't matter.

Some people should never take their caps off.

Or their sunglasses either.

It's what you hear, not what you see.

Your heart has no hair.

Where did all the crew cuts go?

Want Better?

Everybody wants better.

Better cars.

Better homes.

Better money.

Better hair.

We could list a 100 things we want better without effort.

But wanting better is not getting better. Better only happens if you make it happen. It is also best to list wants in order of importance. Whatever you want the most cannot be distracted by the # 2 want. You have to make real headway on #1 to gain the confidence to juggle #2. The world has to see you make progress.

Getting better also requires a real commitment. Real effort. Real pain.

Doubt will attack you. Not quitting will see you through.

Better looks so rosy and perfect and easy to attain. But it ain't.

"Our forefathers wanted better."

Most people want easy better. And then they don't get any "better"....

Look at yourself in the mirror. Do you see better?? Do you see want? Real want?

Everybody can get 'better" if they really work at it. But to get "better" you have to be totally honest for starters, especially with yourself. Then you have to learn respect and manners. Nothing is going to change until you do. Then you have to learn to help others. To get off your "My Horse" and mount the "Your Horse".

Want to make America better again?

Start with the same approach. Be honest and caring.

Demand more from your politicians. Learn more about issues. Make your vote reflect how you feel. Better requires a price from all of us. There will be rough times.

The kid will scream and yell until the "NO" is unwavering. You know it could get nasty, but the easy way is to stand fast. Better is at the end of a tunnel. Don't quit.

Our forefathers wanted better.

They wrote a Constitution.

It was seeded in some 10 Commandments from a long time ago.

Believe in Better.

Quitting is not an option.

Trumpty Dumpty

Everybody loves great falls.

Niagra is the best.

This guy has been beat up so many times but he ain't going over.

Not in his DNA.

Pundits just love to predict the demise of the demisers.

We have to wait and see.

"All the king's horses and all the king's men" doesn't apply here.

Why are stories of failure more fun than success? Do we think we learn more from other's mistakes? Or from our own. Write this guy off too soon, and you won't enjoy the ride or the victory.

It's not that we don't want everyone to do good. Because we do. But we all are our own "Humpty's". And many of us can't be put back together again. Some because of factors way beyond their control, but others because they never learned how not to quit. How to live in Truth and compassion. Attitude destroys too many. Kids hide behind it. The insecure hide behind it. For some it is all they have because they are not being led elsewhere.

"Everybody loves great falls."

So we talk of leadership. Being led somewhere where it is better. Since nobody believes in God anymore we trust some human to do it for us. Not ourselves; which is the tragic caveat.

If you do the same thing all your life you get good at it. If you are a politician you get good at organizing the organizing of decisions. Yielding to bureaucracy becomes the default decision. Is our country a political organization or is it a business or is it a culture... or is it a stroke of luck?

It seems that economic vitality is essential to prosperity and jobs.

So maybe, just maybe... we should roll the dice with a businessman.

Passion trumps politics?

Wallsrus

Think about it.

We have fences around every swimming pool.

We have fences around all our property.

We have fences around government property.

Serious fences to keep terrorists away too.

Sometimes fences work.

We are a nation of accumulation. So much stuff in storage. Ever look into garages these days? No cars, just stuff and a lawnmower.

We are the country of want in so many ways. We want peace and happiness and fast food. We are the country that everybody has a want for.

This jealousy has befuddled the socialist worlds for centuries. Communism, Islam, Fascism create confrontations of frustration. But deadly serious. We cannot dismiss them.

Border control is mandatory for these cultures. But these are often walls of punishment and terror. They are paranoid about

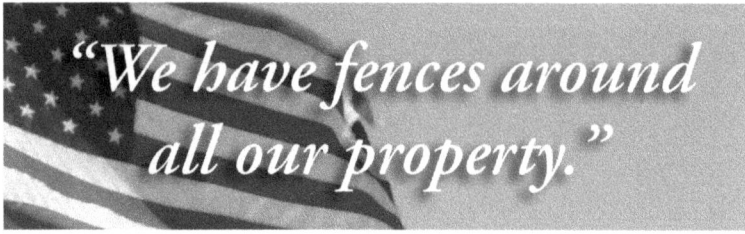
"We have fences around all our property."

western influence. Here we are in the 21st century too!

So we need wall nutrition. Healthier walls to keep potential chaos distant until it can be controlled. Our wellness must be agreed upon. If not?? Why do we have fences around our schools?? Are there not too many simple parallels?

Walls cost money. Everything in life costs money except Trust, Honesty, and Love. We are led to talk about borders. Just to manage and control outside input. Human well-being is in play on both sides of a border. But "NO" must mean no to our children and our borders.

Build the wall. Make it serious. Sensors, computers, drones.... New tools exist. The fat is in a bureaucracy somewhere. A businessman knows expense control and allocation. Hello?

Migration will become immigration once we are known to be serious.

Immigration should respect each individual and the playing field should be fair and orderly.

We have let the status of our illegal get out of control.

Our shame. Families and children and human beings.

Our political acumen never saw it coming?

Or just leave it to the next administration?

Pass the Latino buck?

WALLS'R'US.

Prompter

The first thing you ever heard was probably "coochy coo".

You were being prompted to smile as soon as you were born!

Then growing up there were directions as to how to do whatever.

Right.

Wrong.

All prompts.

You thought it was all over and then you got married.

How do actors become so believable? How do the people on the Today Show seem so smart and perfect? Opinions, ideas, arguments, explanations.... All seem so natural.

Except that they aren't. They aren't real. Though a fortune is spent making them appear real. And we love it. The escape into a movie or HBO Series is dramatic. (pun intended).

Commercials... not real. Testimonies... not real. Oaths... not real. So what is real anymore? The president has his see-

"Special interests prompting congressmen."

thru teleprompters that appear to be nothing. His diction and presentation flows like butter on toast. A verbal symphony. Politician after politician is the same. Talking points overwhelm genuineness. Winks from the side prompting direction.

Special interests prompting congressmen. Everyone is telling everybody else what to say. Brave new world? Brave new prompting. Pretty soon we will have drone prompters.

Billy Graham didn't need prompting. Martin Luther King was pretty good too.

Be mindful that some of the most evil people never needed prompting. In fact all evil people don't need to be told what to say. Terror flows without prompt.

These days most all ask "What do you think?" Social networks are all about the "What do you thinks?". Every opinion from as many people as possible creates consensus and chaos. Indecision prompts indecision. Before we can make a decision we need one more opinion.

Yet America is supposed to be a nation that applauds rugged individualism.

We and congress and ad nauseam... can't make decisions for ourselves.

We have to decide to rebuild our nation and decision making.

What do you think?

Be Strong

To stand up for what is right you have to be strong.

To say no to drugs you have to be strong.

To be a good parent you have to be strong.

To be a good politician you have to be strong.

To be a good citizen you have to be strong.

If you want to be strong you cannot quit.

To be strong you have to have beliefs and believe in them. You have to have values. You cannot wait for them to come to you. You will be uncomfortable but you have to go out and find them. The hard way. On your own. Make mistakes and learn. There is no easy way.

A political campaign is demanding and not comfortable. Questions, travelling, criticism, coffee, beds that are old, schedules, interviews, debates, advice, and a unique aloneness. You gotta be strong or stupid.

You have to stand for something, not sit.

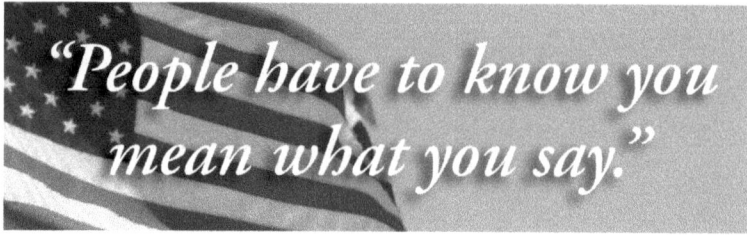

"People have to know you mean what you say."

Be the target. And don't flinch when you hear the trigger. There is always something headed your way. Concocted by others in other places. Wanting to test your strength. Not caring. Just looking for weakness. That's life.

Being strong means admitting that there are forces at play to keep you from being strong. Whispers in your ear that are false. Loyalties that aren't.

At the end of the day is our ability to make a decision on the spot that is a decision and not an equivocation.

The power of the word "NO" is when it is steadfast.

People have to know you mean what you say.

We get all caught up in nuances and sentiments.

The dither in media and politics.

Be strong and say NO to this waste of time.

Put yourself on the podium in all the bright lights and stand for something.

Be strong.

Trumpectomy

How much anesthesia will be required to numb so many bureaucrats?

It's frightening to see the poll percentages.

Why are so many so absorbed with this one guy?

Why do so many elitists raise scorn to a new level?

What level of surgery does our country need for a "Trumpectomy"?

How far has the bureaucratic cancer spread? What will be the recovery period? Will the patient die on the operating table?? Will it be our final hypocrisy to deny what the majority wishes?

The status quo in our nation is obviously unacceptable. It is an irritant to growth. It is an irritant to the common man. There is a comfort imbalance. Less money is being made by more. Serious surgery is needed here... not just exploratory.

We have to carefully choose the surgeon. He better be the Chief Surgeon of the Business Wing. It will be the future health of small business that underpins our future.

Attitudes must change about work. No one is entitled to excessive

"What level of surgery does our country need for a "Trumpectomy"?"

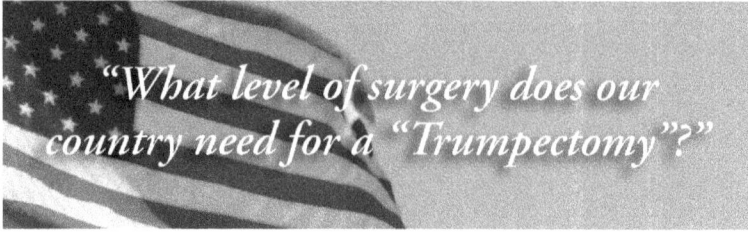

entitlement... From government employees to welfare candidates. Honesty must creep back into the mainstream. Values must be raised and not fine-printed into obscurity. We are a great nation in need of surgery. And not surgery from the forces of evil abroad.

The battle is within. Each of us should look inward and see what falsehood, prejudice, and ignorance we should remove. Respect is the scalpel. Selflessness is the stitches.

Political combat must be exorcised. Parties at war must find peace. Energy must go to unity.

Change the names of the parties from Democrat to Helpocrat and Republican to Agreeican.

Get rid of the jackasses and overweight trunks.

Let their new icons be the Dove and the Cross.

Deal with it.

It is where we came from.

Unless the past never existed…..

Nurse, hand us the spreader.

Donald Duck

"Incoming".....

Everybody hits the ground and covers their head.

Don't want the brain to get a bruise.

How can you tell how many missiles are in the air?

Or drones hovering??

Or the journalists in the shadows being able to say anything without accountability? Is a journalist bias-free?

We are told so many things by so many people, all portending to have the Truth. How do we know what their personal value structure is? Or are they just an amalgam of loaned opinions? Is not the credibility of a person based on how honest, how humble, and how respectful they are? How do we find that out?

The smiley faces on our media screens are after hair, makeup, prompting, and rehearsal. They look us straight in the eye. Beckoning trust. We buy into it.

So duck Donald, the incoming has just begun. Every candidate in history has had the half-truth bomb thrown. The I.O.D., the Improvised Opinion Device.

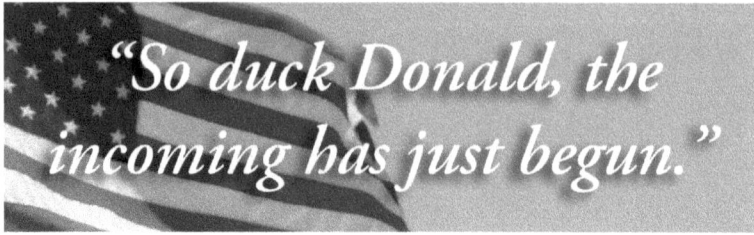
"So duck Donald, the incoming has just begun."

The stands are clapping as you raise your forearms to deflect and defuse the verbal lightning bolts.

Mirror them right back at the sender and see how they can stand the heat. It should all not be one way they say….. Heroes that last find humility and keep finding it. This gives their strengths strength. It is always good to make a mistake and then own up to it. Most dodge and parse their credibility away.

There is always two sides to every nuance. The press has a funny way of always finding the irritating one. Flash bulbs and clicking shutters obscure the moment. Truth cannot be freeze-framed. It has to flow and be exposed to constant scrutiny.

Never duck the incoming question.

Always say "nice question" and then flatten it with Truth.

Truth remains about values.

About good and evil.

Don't be the Donald who ducks.

Hedgehogs

It's getting harder to hide.

Submarines have gotten quieter.

They know how to hide better these days.

In WWII there were these explosive depth charges that were shot out forward.

They had a much better kill record.

Today there are all kinds of detection sensors and sophisticated torpedoes. The chess match is played underwater all around the world. Nuclear tipped persuasion.

Underneath Wall Street are new forms of money manipulation that go on quietly. They have escaped detection by the IRS... The greatest detection agency we have. A befuddled bureaucracy that could not make these profit shufflers pay a fair share. Profit hogs.

Mainstream America is left out of the equation. Yet their backs created the foundation for every company that succeeds. Management and worker alike never see the profit of their toil. Shares in what? Financial sophistication is made from fax and phone alone. No sleeves rolled up and hands dirtied.

"The Hedges hog too much."

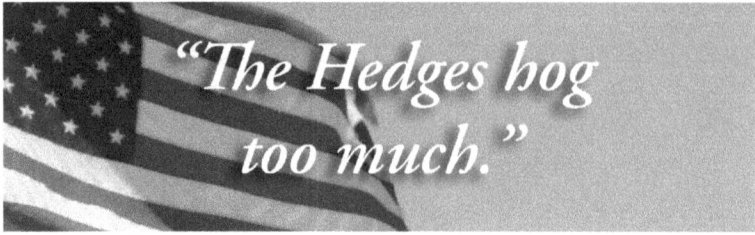

How do you make the system more fair? I have no clue. But it is time for someone to try.

It's not just Hedge Funds… they are just refinements of a financial dynamic that could reward more. These profits can be sent to infrastructure, medical, and job creation. Taxation must be simplified. Government expense must be reduced. Management accountability must not just be a phrase. Civil servants must serve, not shuffle paper. Government is not profitable… Companies which get fat fail.

Entitlement that gets fat fails. Except… there is no way to measure it until it is too late.

The Hedges hog too much. These minds could be profitable in a different sense… for us, not self. They can be part of the solution and not the aggravation.

There is enough need in our nation, much less the world, to keep them busy and their boats at the dock.

So let the pot be stirred.

We can do better.

Cheap Shot

It's all about being cheap.

Buying something that has poor quality.

Doing something that is selfish.

Without a full load a bullet misses its target.

Someone has to pull the trigger.

And pay the consequences.

We all watch television and know what a cheap shot is. They pretend like we don't know. Hello, maybe we are smarter that they are? Because cheap shots mean one is dumb. A price will be paid. And the cheap shot always backfires. We are not the dumb ones.

Cheap shots used to be looked down upon. Now they are committed in the guise of entertainment. Controversy created and ratings satiated.

We are also guilty participants as we sit back and buy larger screens to watch the flow of half-truths. Then we get up and grab a drink during the commercials which subsidize the half-truth.

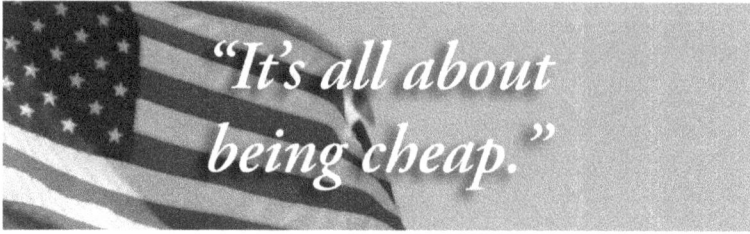

"It's all about being cheap."

The late show comedians then have all the fodder they require to help us laugh at ourselves and the cheap shots.

Pass the tequila Carlos.

Rights Anonymous

What right do I have to be right?

What are the rights of the right?

Does someone else have to be wrong for me to be right?

Do I have to be quiet or do I have my rights?

Is to disagree a right or is it a wrong?

Help me I am so confused about what is right.

Well, first of all, being wrong is not right. Let's repeat it… "Being wrong is not right." There are several types of wrongs. One, the innocent mistake that is just wrong and harms no one. Simple wrong that we dismiss and forgive. No one needs to know and we learn from it.

Then, more importantly, the wrong we know is not a mistake because we knew it was wrong beforehand and did it anyway. Bet this one affected someone else… like in 95% of the time… ok, well… 100% of the time. Damage done, but don't think about it and move on. There are plenty of excuses available.

What right do we have to be wrong? None, absolutely none. If

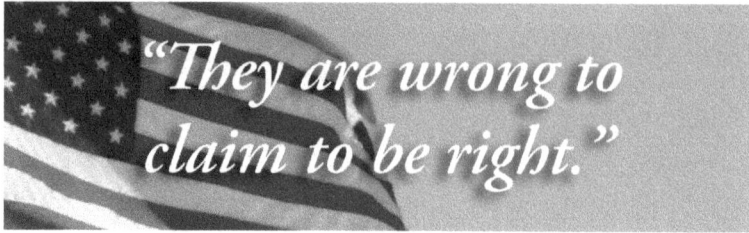

we had listened when told what was right and wrong from the beginning, wrong would have been less desirable. But no, we, us little we's are self-justified and unassailable. Ego, greed, lust, pride, envy, etc. are embraced and forgiven as necessary journeys. They are even celebrated in the gossip magazines....

Ok, now a big leap into this war of rights and wrongs, and.... their rights.

For instance, in the news these days is the predator. What he did is wrong; horribly wrong. There is no excuse for this behavior. Let justice take its course. What right did he have to be wrong? None. Absolutely none.

How can he right his wrong? By being honest with himself, and us, and apologizing for his wrong. By asking for forgiveness. We are capable of listening to this plea.

But what about the wrongs done to those perpetrated against? The victims. Ghastly consideration. But, life does go on and builds from its pain and chaos. Forgiveness becomes the only weapon against all hidden, traumatic hurt. Forgiveness allows guilt to be abandoned. Forgiveness allows the scar tissue to form stronger upon the will and determination of the innocent victim.

One can stand tall again, as can the military veteran who has seen the unseeable.

Pillars of society can emerge from the pain of this chaos to lead us and our children down roads of right. Of right only.

There is a war to be fought against the rights of the wrong. Who can lead if not all of us? Who can be demonstrably vocal against the wrongs in every moment? Who can see the wrong better than those who have been wronged? Let the wronged lead the right back to our rights!

"We have our rights!" is the cry of the masses.

Is it not time that we all came back together and agreed upon what is right and wrong?

We are getting nowhere as we have discarded our traditions and moral roots.

Democrats and Republicans dither over legalities and interpretations.

They send the message that there is nothing right or wrong.

They are wrong to claim to be right.

It hurts.

She Works Hard

"She works hard for the money" is one of my ringtones.

When I hear it I know the person calling really works hard and is alone a lot.

Almost half the year she is gone.

Working hard for the money.

Really hard.

I have been watching The Voice on NBC a lot this year. The new judges are the best yet. They get along and laugh a lot. Their laughter is infectious and makes the show decent.

But what is more intriguing are the backgrounds of the contestants. Most come from families which have had to struggle.

These candidates have humble roots and often have a single parent or have had to work to provide income for their parents. It is so refreshing to see them walk on the stage and offer themselves up for rejection.

I am in awe of the single moms and women who take on more than one job to support their kids, who have pride and think

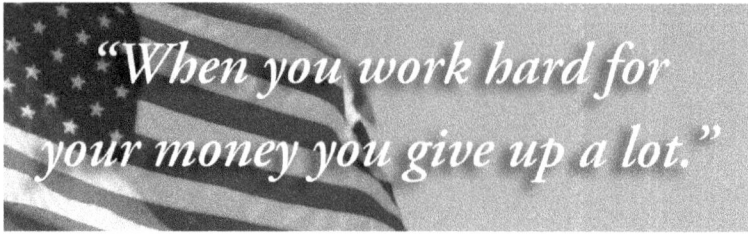

"When you work hard for your money you give up a lot."

beyond entitlement. Those kids are the ones who can truly respect their parents. Because their parents showed leadership and sacrificed their lives unselfishly.

Real leaders.

Real heroes.

Hard work is an understatement.

The lesson here is that there is no substitute for hard work. It allows you to be proud. You earn respect. You do not get it by fancy corporate titling. Like "Associate Executive Service Representative"……. You get it the old fashioned way… That really should be the only fashionable way. LOL

When you work hard for your money you give up a lot. Your peers can be seen as having all the fun and living like life is a party. But in the long run the foundation is rock solid when you work hard. Whether you make a lot or a little, you can hold your head high. When you make a lot, more people are dependent upon you. What an honor.

Money does not have to spoil you if you are not selfish with it.

Make your yacht the well-being of others.

Well earned.

Life with the biggest smile.

And smiling inside too.

VOTE.

Made In America

I was made in America.

I was born in New York.

I was not born in Africa.

I was not born in China.

I was not born in Iran.

I was not born in Mexico.

How come I was not born in Siberia? I don't know. But I'd like to meet the Guy who made the decision and shake His hand.

Why does everyone want to come here? Can't they just leave us alone and solve their own problems. We did ours... Kill off as many of your own as you want. Just leave us alone. We will even provide a little foreign aid for you if you do.

We don't have anything you can't have. Liberty, Justice, and Freedom for all. Just do it. Equality? Human rights? Just words that make such good common sense that everyone understands. Capiche?? So get on with it. Google all you need to structure

"*I was made in America.*"

your country like ours... cast some votes... throw out the bad guys... show women some respect... and be kind to animals... and... you may get even more foreign aid.

Okay America, what the heck is wrong with you? Why are you setting such a bad example to the rest of the world? Great job in managing family without fathers. Great job in legalizing nonsense and pot, metaphorically speaking. Great job in legalizing the legalizing of everything so fine print is your new god. Great job in idol worship at the expense of value worship.

Yet everyone still wants to be 'Born in the USA'... (Thanks Bruce). Go figure.

Now we used to give birth to all kinds of products in the USA... But somewhere greed took over and managements in both business and labor started to get paid much more than they should. The rest is history. But everyone wants to become an American citizen. (I hope it is not for the entitlements...)

You know we put a man on the moon. I just bet we could build factories in our homeland and put man back to work. I just bet CEO's could make it happen if their bonuses were at stake. And, by the way, they aren't the bad guys, they are the good guys... if they would reconnect with their values. Their leadership is essential. But they must work alongside the worker, shoulder to shoulder, to build mutual respect.

Ask a veteran how it works.

Ask a Navy SEAL how it works.

Made in America.

Heck, let's make everything in America.

Let's make pride and trust and teamwork more than chalk on a Harvard blackboard.

Judge and Jury

This is going to be so much fun.

I know none of you have ever been judgmental.

You have never looked down on anyone regardless of how they looked or acted.

I am sure your face always reflected impartiality and understanding.

There are other cultures and persuasions. There are other interpretations of right and wrong. I know you feel uncomfortable as soon as you feel an opinion forming. You are an enlightened citizen who never judges what the media or others might. Whenever you read a text criticizing someone you withhold judgment… while admonishing the sender for pre-judging. You are just good. In fact, you are perfect. There is no wrong until a fair and carefully selected jury decides. In time, in due course.

The problem is that we have constructed a courtroom in our own head. We never tell anyone, but we are the Chief Justice of Our Own Supreme Court that comes to order whenever requested. This can be characterized as "headstrong"… or "headwrong"???

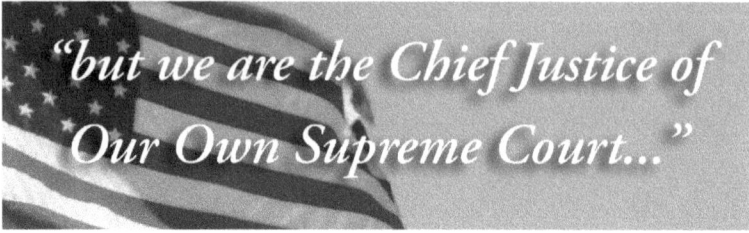
"but we are the Chief Justice of Our Own Supreme Court..."

Gossip and scandal help condition us to instant decision, instant jury ruling. There are no recesses allowed. We move quickly from one tidbit to another accruing decisions and sentences before our mind's ink is dry. Yes we all know it is our nature to judge all day long. Jury selection not needed. Just let me see someone and I have an instant opinion and it is soon cemented by texting. Judge and Jury… that is who we are until we close the court and open our heart.

Did we know all the circumstances about that person? Never. Do we want to be judged without a jury? Never. Do we want to be able to correct a judgment against us? You bet.

To be judged fairly we have to start by judging fairly. We have to be known as a very principle-driven, honest person. We have to be known for only caring about Truth. We have to be known for only caring about others. We have to be known for being humble.

Tall order.

"Court is now in session."

"Would the accused please rise?"

Yes, all of you. Yes, all of humanity.

Yes, you Presidents, Kings, and CEO's too."

"You are all found guilty of judging one another".

"Sentencing will be next Wednesday after you have all read the Bible."

Poll Results

The campaigns are over.

The poll results are in.

Nobody likes you.

Ok the majority doesn't like you.

You are not giving interviews.

How do we get enough opinions from others to know where we stand? Have we spent enough money with the right people to get us the results we wanted? We wanted to win. We wanted everybody to like us. Damn, we tried so hard.

We have raised poll taking to a science.

Nothing is done any longer without a poll to give the enlightened decision makers courage to act. Gut instincts have been totally discredited. Your singular opinion has been totally discredited. Gallup polls, Harris polls, CNN polls, Nielson ratings.... All making big money out of asking stupid questions of thousands to build their databases with assuredness. But... a lot of us answer in shaded manners, interpret differently..... polls can be wrong. You can lose your job with the wrong poll information.

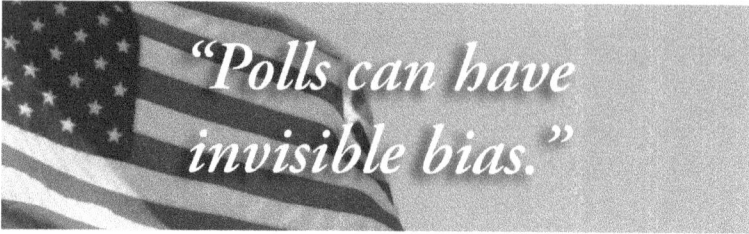

Polls can have invisible bias.

We have taken morality out of schoolbooks and classrooms. No polls taken in conservative demographics. Morality is prejudicial. No, hard core, unbiased statistics guide the money flows. Ha! Wanna bet on it? Only as honest as the CEO…. And we want them scandal free and church abiding leaders. Ain't happenin'.

So back to living, guided by the feelings of others as we interpret them… Feelings are driving most everything these days. Poll the feelings and you have a winner.

Tilt. Bad people have feelings. Evil has no feelings. Very complicated.

There has to be a time when there is no time for polls.

Triggers have to be pulled.

The terrorist may just have to be shot.

We can take polls afterwards as to how we feel.

But at least my head was not cut off.

My heart knew what made sense.

I shot him when the polls were closed.

Poverty

Nobody wants their kids to be poor.

We hold them when nursing so they feel wanted.

We clothe them and feed them and nurture them so they feel secure.

We watch them closely so they acquire feelings and understandings that we hold important.

We know a little of what poverty can be like and we try to shield our children with education and positive activities.

We do our best.

Then they are on their own. The world is never as they expect it. We put them in the raft, then push it out into the current in the river of life to take them where it will.

If the river is in the United States, there is hope. But suppose your river is in Syria, Ethiopia, Yemen, North Korea, Iran, Egypt, Saudi Arabia, or even Russia or China? Try and put yourself in those kid's shoes... if they have any. Maybe you should teach your own kids about the real world beforehand; her history and her poverties.

"Nobody wants their kids to be poor."

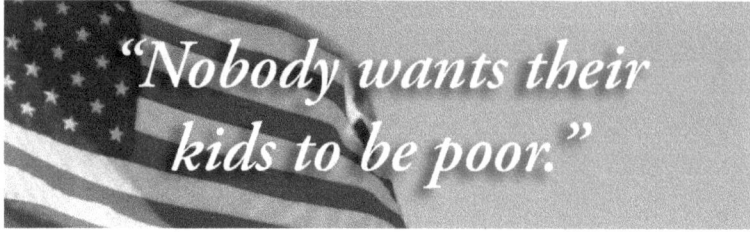

Socialist states create massive entitlement mindsets and stifle individual potential.

More and more people are turning to government to provide work and easy compensation and insurance.

Bureaucracies become inefficient cancers.

Reaching critical mass, the majorities feel entitled and the society crumbles.

Poverty kills.

Entitlement kills.

Our kids are getting spoiled. There is a digital culture that is providing instant gratification. Keyboards are rewarding impulse and that is leading to entitlement. Parents are being expected to continue providing for everything and future security. Entitlement is becoming the arrogance of the ignorant. Woe to us all.

No one is entitled to anything other than liberty, freedom, and fairness. Look at all the countries where this is an illusion and a lie. What are your odds of getting anything if you are black, female, and born in the Middle-East?

Your mother's love is the only brief glimpse of fairness you will ever see.

You are entitled to nothing other than depravation, pain, and uncertainty.

We should send all our kids over there again in a new Peace Corps, but call it Fight Poverty Corps.

Tell it like it is.

Serious Politics

Now this is a funny chapter.

The hard part will be not laughing out loud. LOL

Now it is very easy to criticize politicians these days.

The House, the Senate, the Governor, the secretary of this and that, and even the White House. They have asked for it and they got it. LOL. Except we voted for each one of them. LOL

The world is spinning out of control with the evil in other governments. Yes, Evil with a capital E. We won't admit it. We use words to parse it away. New phrases and categories to make it seem benign. Shit people... Evil is evil! It is not a war on anything else. Evil is created by pride, vanity, selfishness, power, and poverty. Injustice is rampant. The abuse of women and children is astounding. Yet we indulge in meaningless protest and jabbermouthing. We act like we don't want politics to get serious as we rush from one fire to another. Ebola is symbolic of everything that is out of control.

Kids mouthing off. Respect for family and authority going down the drain. Respect for all that we have built in this great

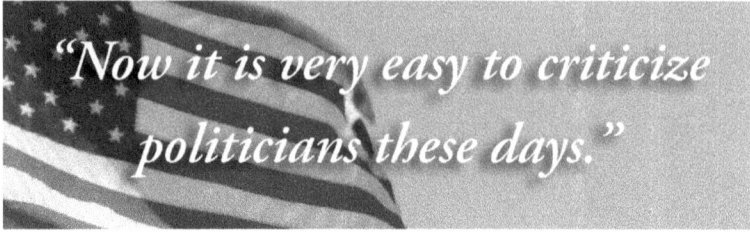

nation is under assault. The media observes and turns it into entertainment.

Who is laughing out loud? We had better answer that question. What red line has been crossed? Do we have any red lines?? Do you personally have any red lines anymore? What are they? Are you willing to tell someone else and risk criticism? Do we stand for anything?

Serious politics requires serious politicians.

Serious politics requires serious voters.

This is no laughing matter.

Unequal Equals

All men were created equal as affirmed by us on July 4, 1776.

It is easy to say.

But we know there are so many people who do not deserve this consideration.

Even some who should just be shot.

Everyone has their own list.

This "equal" stuff is a little antiquated. People have yachts and fly around in private jets and others miss payments on their car. For the most part those at the bottom work harder than those on the top.

Of course you can get ahead with hard work and commitment. But those opportunities are getting more elusive. We may have developed a systemic inequality where a significant percent are guaranteed relative poverty, or certainly limited access to the middle class. And where the middle class can only lookup and hope .....

Politicians and preachers today tell us we are all equal..... but how?

Where is the leader who can bring us together both morally and "opportunityally" (like the new word?)

"Is inequality institutionalized?"

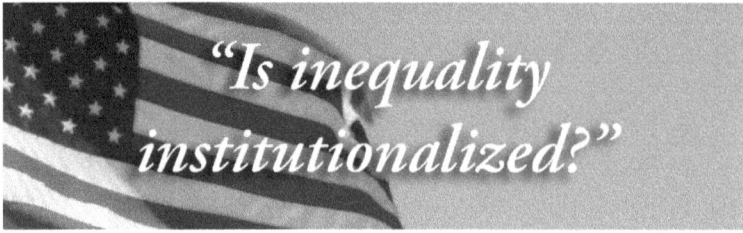

A leader who can remold bureaucracy to serve rather than self-administer. Who can make bonuses really taxable? Who can transparently attack inefficiency and inequality? Who can redefine entitlement in a way that is honest and focused on the real needy, not on those who know how to play the system?

Laziness can no longer be protected by the system.

You can't make decisions behind a desk.

You can't make decisions based upon layers of approvals.

Someone must look someone in the eye and make a judgement... Someone must accept responsibility for a decision.

It must no longer be easy to pass the buck. Delay because of administrative requirements is a scam.

July 4, 1776 was meant to make us honest and equal. Lives were lost fighting for this nation to be free. In every war. Now we are losing more lives from inequality than war.

"We hold these truths to be self-evident, that **all men are created equal**, that they are endowed by their Creator with certain unalienable Rights,...."

Have we lost our way?

Is inequality institutionalized?

"Creator?"

You kidding me??

Supreme Tort

We finally have the final word from the Supreme Court.

Thank God we have somewhere to go to find out what is right and wrong so we can get back to our daily lives.

Awaiting their decisions is so exciting as simplicity can be re-established as a cure for the complexities of having a family and growing a business and just having fun.

When things are so much clearer or clarified there will be a better understanding of the rules of life and getting along. Sometimes a current law needs to be tweaked to make both sides happy.

We call the citizens we send to Washington our lawmakers. They debate and decide on how to make our lives so much better and we are always anxious to celebrate their success.

But it is all a filibuster on our freedoms as our lives have been put on hold by layers of lawyers litigating liberally.

I am so glad we have a Supreme Tort... oops... I mean Supreme Court... sorry....

They are the professional arbiters of laws and their simplification.

We can relax.

The question is…..????

Why are we making laws about laws faster than McDonalds can sell Big Macs…?

We have a cause, a right, or a wrong, and we demand new laws to protect and insure that only good will prevail. But as soon as a law is passed you can bet there is a law in waiting to better define the law in question. So we are better defining everything to the point of??? Who cares?? Who cares about the laws? They are so complicated that they are ignored…until somebody complains and sues….and sues… and sues…..

I have a right to sue is the birth child of all the laws.

I was asked to sign a simple contract for airing a commercial. The rate and price was simple. I signed as agreed. They called back and said I had not signed the terms of acceptance. Ok… So I go look again at the 4 pages of fine print I was supposed to rubber stamp and trust them. It would cost me a pretty penny to have my attorney review it and then get back to their attorney. I said shove it. Cancel the spot. In fact, it is insulting that they ask us to sign fine print without their paying for your attorney to review it. Hello??? We abrogate our rights. Oh, by the way, they called back and said everything was ok. They would run the spot.

Our existence has been "fine printed". That is why the word "whatever" has become a philosophy in its own. Fine print is everywhere lurking in the shadows ready to hold you responsible....

We need to be *tortified* or *detorted* or something. We are being torted to death by our own laws. We are being wronged by our laws. Admittedly we need laws...but there is a limit. Where is the "I can't Take It Anymore Movement"??? Maybe it is time to move west again and farm my own land... say 3-4 acres.... Get some ducks and a horse...and a gun.... Like they did when they came over here from England. LOL.

What ever happened to tort reform?

Weren't we working on making frivolous or unfair lawsuits illegal?

Lawsuits that were made easy by laws?

Yes tort reform.....

Kinda got lost in all the international crisis attention, and all the economic stagnation debate, and all the political negative excitement.

I mean really lost.

Well, at least we have the Supreme Tort.

Rights Abuse

Let's form a new special interest group, the SPCR.

The Society for the Prevention of Cruelty to Rights.

I am so sick and tired of rights being abused, watered down, and used as issues against the majority.

Whew… this is really dangerous terrain…

Let's amend the Right to have Rights. Let's define that the majority oppresses all minority interests and feelings. Let us raise the smallest group of like-minded to decide the rights of all who feel differently. There is no more room for good unless it is the minority. Where nothing has value unless it has no value. Bet I got you with this… LOL.

We can make anything legal that we want … unless, of course, it is opposed by a sincere self-interest group.

Sounds like chaos?? Well, step back… and let's be honest… absurdity is approaching.

If your values are not mine, then yours are wrong. I am so thankful we have a Supreme Court to help us decide if our rights

"We have become slaves to rights."

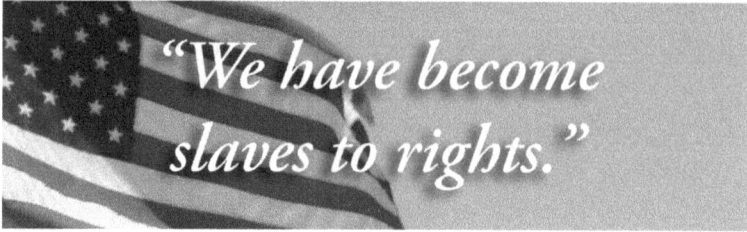

are right. But all it takes is one vote to the contrary and my rights are wrong. Is that right? For one person to decide the fate of another?? Much less a majority?? Of course you have the right to say that I am wrong, but I have the right to get a ruling that you are wrong. And the SPCR is behind me! Unless they think I am being cruel to your rights... LOL.

If my wife wants to shop at midnight on Sundays who has the right to deny her shopping rights. Aren't her feelings and needs important too??

What is a right?

Can some court define it better??

I have a right to fight for her rights.

We need Lincoln back.

We have become slaves to rights.

100 Million

Now... I know you have no clue where this is going.

100 Million is a big number...

Maybe it's the age of our planet?

Maybe it is the number of people killed in our lifetime?

Maybe it is the number of burgers sold in California in a month??

Maybe it is the number of divorces on record?

Let's all make lists of things that relate to the number 100 million....

Well, the big number is how much waste we can achieve with so little effort. Environmentalists take note! Yes, carbon emissions kill, but so does money wasted by us all that could serve better purposes... like world hunger.

Well it so happens that in the great state of North Carolina in the year of our Lord 2014... 100 million dollars was spent on the election for Senator of the United States. Democratic and Republican Parties were spending that much trying to defeat the other. Shame on all of us that we have risen so low.

"Maybe it is the number of burgers sold in California in a month??"

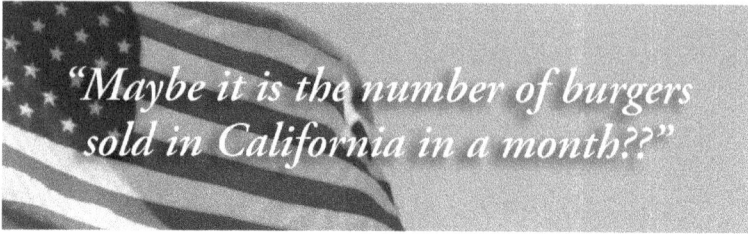

We have a system of laws and regulations meant to control outside influence that have created infinite opportunities for abuse. Our politicians are not protecting our nation. They just play at politics in the sandbox called Washington.

Where are leaders with vision?

Where are leaders who stay their course rather than bend with the wind?

Moral certitude? Abandoned. Mocked. Neutered.

Sometimes I wish media would show steadfast commitment to our time-tested values and morays. Is it asking too much? Our schools are bending to sentiment and feelings and political correctness… We are digging cultural ditches beyond our imagination. Our civilization is finding more reasons to disagree than to agree.

Laughter is no longer funny.

Laughter is fake when all else is chaos.

Maybe it is time for a Leader to return.

57 Virgins

Why do men want so much?

Back in the beginning of civilization or even existence, the male of our species was the provider and protector.

He was in charge of life and death, rules and punishment.

The woman was in charge of birth, nurturing, and pleasure.

Over the millenniums more and more rules were established to protect order and fragile justice. Life was tribal, then cultures formed creating new interpretations of old rules.

Not all that much fine print on scrolls? Men fought the wars. Killed off enough to rule for a while until the cycle repeated itself.

Woman was always second and mainly voiceless. Pleasure for the male was insured by laws...harsh laws... which still stand in significant parts of the world today. Look at the headlines.

Women's rights are still at a standstill in Africa, the Middle-East, and the Orient..... It ain't right. Meanwhile we dither about our glass ceilings...

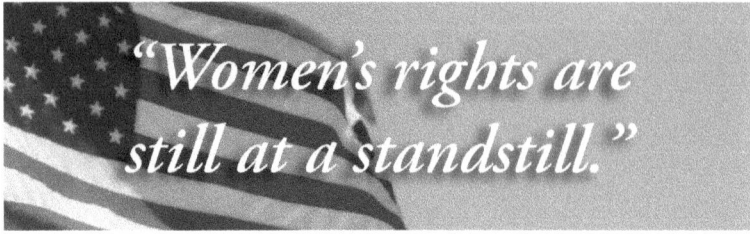
"Women's rights are still at a standstill."

I don't need to be promised 57 virgins to go to heaven. That is sexist too. I don't dream about flopping around naked on clouds in exotic heavenly pleasures. Anyone who promises such is lying.

I just want the assurance I get to see my Mom and Dad again... And get to know their parents, and their parent's parents.

I believe I cannot kill anyone if I want to get there.

I believe I have to ask for forgiveness to qualify.

I want to be able to receive forgiveness from all who I had hurt. It may take a little time... but that would be heaven to me.

Rules should be made for human beings, not genders.

They should all be updated and simplified so they can easily be texted and shared on Facebook.

Get governments out of the rule business.

It seems like they are adding amendments and qualifications weekly.

Who can keep track of all the fine print?

Sign here....

And be held accountable in cyber-space for eternity.

Oops... I didn't read the fine print.

It is only 2 old virgins.

Muslim Sunglasses

Do you know they are making sunglasses that work with the burqa?

You can hardly see the eyes as it is.

Talk about becoming mysterious….

More dark, more intriguing.

Hey… what is the point of being a woman if no one can look at you?

When there is bright sun and SPF is required, the sunglass industry is right there for any price you wish to pay. Try a Chanel for $300? Why?? Do you really see better? I think sunglasses are more fashion than required unless, of course, you are climbing Mt Everest or flying an F35 into the dawn.

Tints make what one sees unnatural. It is like we don't want to see things for what they really are. N'est-ce pas??

We are being drawn into cultural assimilations that just are not the U S of A. Talk about a clash of cultures!!! Beverly Hills bikinis vs burqas in a steel cage match. Nothing to grab on the LA Divas

"You can hardly see the eyes as it is."

and everything to grab on the champion burqa feline. You can't train in burqa... but you can do everything in a bikini... LOL

What in the world are we going to do with this Muslim thing?

I know we are supposed to be politically correct. But radical Islam is giving the whole Muslim world a bad image. Really bad. Fear is their weapon and we are afraid of fear.

Ask us to be forgiving... we like to forgive. But WWII started off just this way. It took Churchill and Roosevelt to face fear's ugly face and give us resolve and hope.

Our worlds came together.

Evil had united us.

Good won.

Nobody tried to avoid the draft.

What are we looking for from our government? Yes, we run there more and more these days to solve all our problems. They can only come up with legislation. Haven't we all had enough with legislation? There is so much that only an extra-terrestrial can figure it out. LOL

Maybe we all should wear a burqa so the bad guys can't see us?

I'm gonna wear sunglasses.

Are there any 6 foot Muslim women?

Last Party

You are only as good as your last party.

The next day you got to tell everyone about it and you were the center of "happeningness".

Your friends hung on your every word. You were happy. You were what was happening.

Probably was a Saturday night. Hello Sunday morning realities. Kids gotta do this and that. Forget church. Husband takes off hunting or golfing or something. Sunday dinner choices loom. The Monday commute and work comes too soon.

The mind wanders to the next party. At the party everything seems so much fun. There is no heaviness of responsibility at the party. It can become addictive. Maybe you will pass on the next one if the right people are not coming. Maybe....

Then there is the Republican Party shooting itself in the foot.

Then there is the Democratic Party making targets for the Republican Party.

Nobody gets along at these parties... LOL.

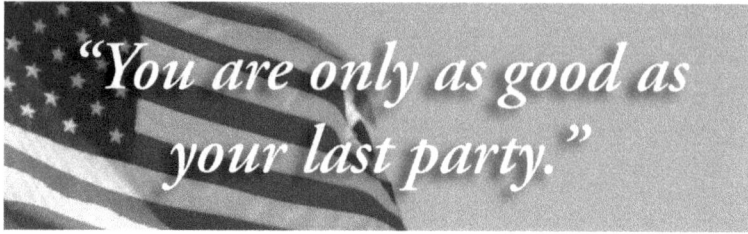

I think we need to discuss the Unified Party at the next party. At these parties everybody gets along and it is so much more fun. Fun. Isn't that what life is all about??

But when one reads about the truly important people in life, one does not hear of parties or fun… They are engrossed in their visions, their work, or helping others. I wish we could talk to them about fun. They had to like what they did, or why do it? And if you were the "best" it had to be fun. Not sports heroes or celebrities, but people who really made a difference. I think that would be a great class for schools. Define and agree on who was really great. How did they benefit man? Once their names are decided upon, find out about their families. Find out how they had fun.

Did they ever throw a party?

What was their last party like?

You are only as good as your last party.

Boundaries

Boundaries are made to help us know what our land is and what someone else's is.

There is usually a fence along the boundary of the property which clearly shows all where your land is.

Out west there is barbed wire, on borders tall fences.

Sometimes boundaries are rivers or oceans. Countries are so defined.

Then again in some wildernesses or deserts there are no fences and the boundary is not visible. Now you don't want to cross over the border boundaries of some countries like North Korea or Iran for fear you might just go right to jail. Pain included.

In another sense, age can be a boundary or a limit to what one can do. Intelligence can be a boundary as ignorance can limit one's journey. Race can be a boundary as it limited movement in our past. Religion sets all kinds of limits that people can either follow or ignore. Much to talk about.

Regardless, boundaries define much of all we can do. If we choose to ignore them then someone will charge us with trespassing and

criminal behavior. If we don't have the better lawyer we can end up in a small room with bars on the window and crummy food… and even torture…

So boundaries are important. Yes??

But then nobody, much less young people, wants someone else telling him what to do or where not to go.

So who respects boundaries these days??

There certainly are no moral boundaries anymore. All you have to do is click the box saying you are over 18 and there are no boundaries. Or click the box Parental Supervision Recommended and whooosh… all boundaries disappear and your fantasies are in high definition.

What about language? There are so many new words that are not yet in the dictionary that we can talk without boundaries or respect for others, much less ourselves.

Now we ask and allow our government to redefine our boundaries all the time. They love to do it. The politics of legislation. Moreover, we want them to do it! Then blame can be meted out to all those who do not respect the regulations, laws, and ordinances. We don't have to worry about what is right or wrong. It is already codified or written into law.

However, with so many laws it is no longer easy to discern boundaries. We need lawyers to help us. Fine print protects all but us. Voice prompts keep us from crossing communication boundaries. Where are we?

I have come across a fantastic Cuban family where all they know is boundaries and discipline. Where "NO" was the operative word, not "Yes".

Work ethic, respect, quality behavior, abnormal intelligence, and logic abound in their sons. Punishment was the reward tor trespass.

This family has their next generation prepared for reality not fantasy. To me they are the new American model.

Boundaries are great. The right ones.

If we wish to be great again we might try to get back to those oldest 10 boundaries…

They are in the No.1 best-selling book of all times.

Click and you can download it.

We the Free

Surrounded by ocean.

We are set free from the worries of tyranny.

Few have a clue of what we had to do.

To create this paradise for you and for me.

Guns sounded.

Sailors "drownded".

In wars across the sea… for we the free.

Our borders are water.

Sometimes it is healthy to put on the other shoe.

Try someone else's to see how it fits and feels.

Suppose your neighbor just wanted to kill you.

And the border is just a line in the sand?

Oh, to be free of that chance.

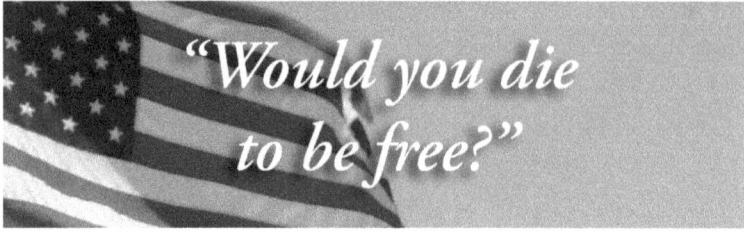

"*Would you die to be free?*"

But we are, don't you see?

We are not Israel.

It is just you and me.

Would you die to be free?

Constitution

My constitution is fine.

I am feeling better.

I am a lot older and had heart surgeries but have really changed my diet and exercising again.

I feel surprisingly good.

My constitution is back to normal.

Less alcohol, less white bread, less sugar, less eating….. It works.

What we do with ourselves determines our constitution. How we feel about ourselves. If we remain centered in self, we just will not feel good, even though we pretend otherwise. The best and only food for a good constitution is helping others. Each time you try it you will like it.

There are rules if you want to feel good, if you want to have a good constitution. There has to be some church with some pastor who can resonate with you. Try to find him or her. Don't quit. Don't prejudge. It is its own arrogance.

We need healthy and wise citizens to lead us out of our bickering

"My constitution is fine."

political chaos. We need to stop amending our Constitution so it is more politically correct. The spirit of our Constitution has served us more than well. There is nothing wrong with it. Fine print cures nothing.

Our founding fathers used Christian principle as our cornerstones. History affirms its solidity. We have fought so many wars trying to protect the inalienable rights we hold dear. We are going to have to fight again soon. Islam rejects our values and culture. We have to stop debating otherwise. We can live in peace only when Islam chooses to champion peaceful co-existence.

Their leaders have to show some leadership or the price paid will be high.

Where is their Constitution that affirms inalienable rights?

And respect and freedom for women.

What century do they live in?

We need peace and honesty for all.

Evil must be recognized for what it is.

EVIL.

Too Bad

Somebody said "Too Bad" to me once and it hurt my feelings.

I can't remember how young I was.

Maybe my Dad said it when I wanted to take the car out when I was 15.

Chris, NO….

But Dad… Please…???

No!

You are not nice Dad! …

"TOO BAD".….

When you are a kid there is something final about a "too bad".

These days you have to be very careful what you say around anyone and everyone. There are so many groups, causes, constituencies, and whatever that have emphatically defined their boundaries, borders, and bruises…. I dare not even mention one for fear of being accused of being an enemy or selfish or antagonistic or anti their "just" position.

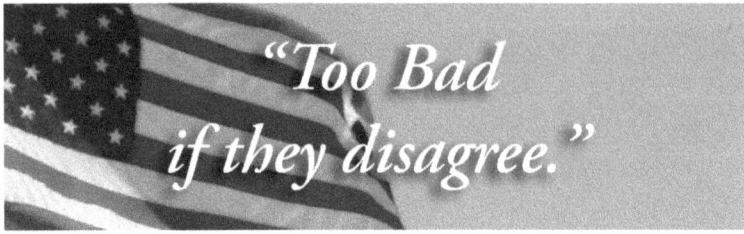

As you read a paper these days someone is accusing someone of terrible thinking or deeds. It is all about accusing. When you accuse, the other person is forced on the defensive and will appear partially defeated. Shrewd tactics. Even better is to wage a silent whisper campaign behind someone's back. By the time they find out, the damage is done.

I think we should rename all causes and parties to one name.

How about renaming the Republican Party to the IDP, the I Disagree Party.

How about renaming the Democratic Party to the IDP, the I Disagree Party.

How about renaming the Occupy Wall Street Movement to the IDM, the I Disagree Movement.

In fact we could do this to most every cause or movement where both sides are vehement. Would simplify things and the evening news could move on to trying to find its roots in truth, good, and constructive news. Let's report more good. Let's focus on collaborative solutions, not boring disagreement. Let's take the talking heads off our TV screens until they can agree.

I know that is a little harsh. I know that some of you disagree and are hitting the delete button. Aw shucks. What do I do? I think I say "Too Bad" and get on with getting on.

Now we can write letters to the editor. Oh, and by the way, how about all the editors coming up with hair splitting logic that helps us wade through the sea of disagreement discourse? Most only offer politically correct "observations" or opinions. You know, this fear of hurting someone else's feelings has gotten out of hand. Now ... do I hear a faint "amen" out there???

We have become obsessed with what others think of us.

We even think we know what others are thinking about us! We have become a culture of chameleons adapting to the *perceived* feelings of others! We have given up our unique identities by constantly being on the defensive in fear of criticism or unflattering opinion.

Again, are there not values or rights or wrongs that we stand for?

Is there no longer anything unequivocal? How can you be you if you can no longer say no? How can you be you if you let your kid use the video game rather than throwing the ball with you outside??

"NO" has to be taken out of the dictionary and put back into our vocabulary.

"NO" defines you. Objections are to be welcomed with a "TOO BAD". TOO BAD can free one from the tyranny of the feelings and opinions of others. Why do we think we need everybody to like us? Why are we glued to our cell phones while missing the clouds and stars above…? Why can't we say what is right reflexively? Too Bad if they disagree. Too Bad.

I wanted to write something that hurt some feelings so I could say "too bad".

But if you agree with me then I can't say it.

Maybe I just want us to agree that disagreeing has gotten out of hand.

Agree or disagree?

Ice Water

If you cut a hole in the ice in the middle of a lake, build your shelter, and sit with your son with your lines going down into the ice water......

Do you think about what in the heck could live there??

Fish.

Cold blooded fish.

Kinda crazy.

And we know that there are cold blooded evil people and governments that are warm blooded. They think nothing about killing. They have to be dealt with. Not ignored.

Sanctions are fine, but sometimes a trigger is required. Drones are sloppy, telescopic sights are better. It takes bravery and courage to get that close.

Dumping buckets of ice water on the heads of celebrities for a noble cause accomplished its mission. I am sure they were so chilly and inconvenienced for a brief moment.

"You don't want to know real cold."

There are significant noble causes that just do not grab our attention enough. Women's and child abuse are at the top.

There is poverty. There is evil…

Only churches are allowed to talk about evil. It is a taboo word outside of those walls. Crazy…when our #1 problem is evil. We just assign it other names so it fades away into politically correct irrelevancy.

Real cold makes you think.

I remember trying to get our rubber boat (IBL Inflatable Boat Large) over an ice covered rock jetty in a snow storm in February 1964. Now that was Navy SEAL training. Now that was evil. LOL. Made for good swearing.

You don't want to know real cold. The ice bucket isn't real cold. We know how to bundle up to avoid it.

Ever read Nathaniel Hawthorne's The Scarlet Letter??

Maybe each of us should carry an ice water bucket around with us all day.

When we start to think about doing something selfish, inconsiderate, or even so slightly evil…

We should stop and dump the bucket on our head as a reminder for all to see...

A reminder that every time we sin our world gets colder.

The Mother Lode

In the mid 1800's in the Sierra Nevada of California there was an enormous migration of entrepreneurs with picks and shovels racing to find eternal happiness and security in the wealth of a giant vein of gold in the hills.

And the California Gold Rush was on.

Tents became towns.

The scream of "Eureka" became new word in our vocabulary, resonating around the world.

It was as if all problems would be solved. Money was the root of all peace not evil. Or that was what one believed, what one hoped, what one had faith in.

Life was not easy in those days. No phones. No computers. No movies. No TV. Just guns and whiskey.

Fighting broke out. Fortunes were stolen. It was the Wild West. No laws. No regulations. No codes. No tax man. No 27,000 page tax code. No lawyers. No media.

Hope turned to tragedy as the latecomers piled into the instant

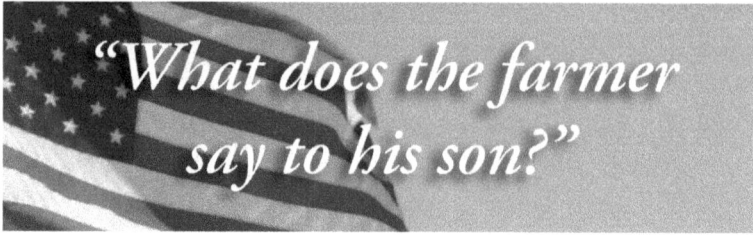

"What does the farmer say to his son?"

cities. Evil became good or vice versa. This mother lode became temporal. But if you stand back… look at the power it had.

Tens of thousands came from Latin America, Europe, and China. San Francisco grew from 200 residents in 1846 to 36,000 in 1852. Billions of dollars of gold was amassed by a few. Most went home with what they started with. Railroads were built. Claims were staked. 100,000 native Indians died… 4,500 murdered.

The mother lode was the mother of much pain.

False hopes? Dead end streets? Rumor driven expectations of fulfillment?

There are all kinds of other Mother Lodes in life, all promising happiness and relief from pain. There are the excesses of drugs and alcohol. There the joys of sex beckoning destruction. There is the distraction of self. There is the trap of social media. Our new world is full of disguised answers to nowhere.

How did we get this far? Hopes dashed. Endless conflict. Endless arguing. Endless war.

There remains the Mother Lode everyone searches for after all others have failed. But we are so stubborn. We are so sure of ourselves. We are so unable to give up ourselves. We are so unable to take advice. Over and over we fight our innate call to good.

We cannot look around and take heed from what is strong, from what is right, from what is unselfish. The thought of being willing to give up control is abhorrent. Don't tread on me. Don't tell me what to do. Then why do we go to school but to learn? To be told what to do? Why do we accept training? Why does a gun require training to not abuse? Why does a child need forceful direction?

Why do we turn away from words like values and truth as if they were ultra conservative radical affronts? Who defines what these days? Is truth only in legislation?

Are we not cable of standing for the simplicity of moral courage and sacrifice? Can we not applaud the soldier of war and of values?

What does the farmer say to his son? "Listen to me son. Work hard every day. Protect your family. Do not sin. Always tell the truth. Show respect to others. Be humble. Embrace forgiveness. Love your mom. Do these and you are my son."

The Mother Lode today is a return to the values that made us strong and unique.

To our Constitution and our Bible.

The Mother Lode is the Cross.

Silence

Silence.

Shhhh…

"You are on silence".

Remember when your teacher or parent used to tell you that?

Or….. "You be quiet or else!….."

Quiet. Silence. Peace.

In the stillness of quiet one begins to listen…. One begins to hear…….

We are talking so much these days…. Okay… texting… Facebooking… Skyping… etc…. in silence… but it really is a roar. Fake silence…. But it is funny if you stand back and see how busy we are being silent…..

Does this new silent world order portend growth and solution or problems…??

Something to think about?

On another note, and more damning is the silence of cowardice.

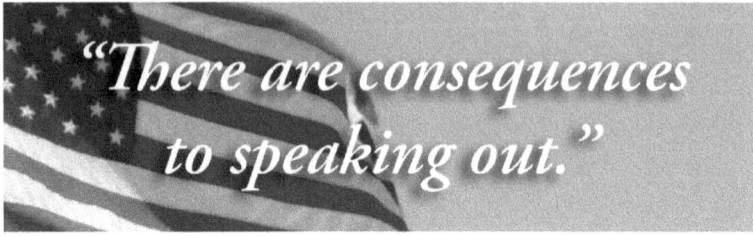

"There are consequences to speaking out."

We can busy ourselves with keyboard activities and not see what is going on around us. We can be brilliant on the small screens that we carry, play, and communicate with… but…. But… Will it be the new battleground of truth … *Or*… Will it be the new battleground avoidance???

At some point our voices have to be heard by ears and action. By vote and reform. The silent majority must be heard out LOUD!!!

Maybe there can be a new government agent called SMD, the Silence Management Directorate? It will advise us when we can and cannot be silent.

I know we all know when we turn our head the other way. When we remain silent about something we prefer to ignore. Or something we wished did not happen. Or something which was not right.

"Don't get involved" is the common rationale. Avoid confrontation… avoid sharing your opinion. Do we know that we have become an avoidance culture?

We have chosen to let others decide what is appropriate. We have gotten our PHD's in sensitivity to sensitivity. A doctorate in inaction.

Silence is becoming our cultural solution to discomfort. In the process, silence is sanctioning chaos.

When all choose not to speak out for values and what they truly believe in, evil and injustice will determine the laws and their interpretation.

The question is what kind of silence do I choose to stand for? What are the consequences of individual silence?

There are consequences to speaking out. Courage and conviction are required.

Name 3 causes. Pick any. List them. Then see which you are not afraid to speak out about.

Your silence will say a lot about who you really are and who you have chosen to be.

Your silence sanctions.

It becomes tacit approval by you of what kind of abuses....?

You decide.

Say Something

"Say something, I'm giving up on you" are lyrics from a wonderful song of the day.

What does it mean beyond a broken love relationship?

Beyond the song?

Our nation was founded on principles that were hammered out by a group of men with a united vision. They didn't want things to be the way they were. They envisioned freedom and justice for ALL. Absolutely no laughing matter.

In our new journey into political correctness, polarization, negative advertising, and accusation it seems as if everyone is guilty until proven otherwise..... yes... right here in the USA.!

The polls indicate our intentions before any vote. Smear and fear are on the front pages. One may be afraid to go to the polls to vote for fear of violence?? What is terrorism but the creation of fear?? Radical this or radical that, murder is murder and deserves no leniency.

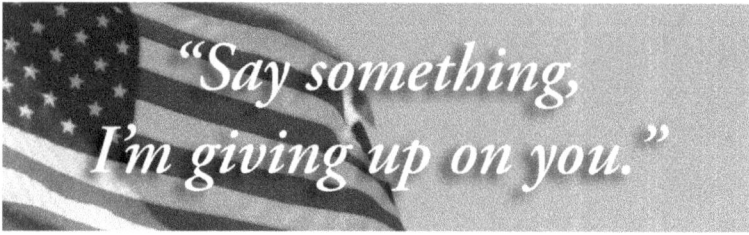

"Say something,
I'm giving up on you."

When did we become so sensitive that the murderer can have his own radio show from prison??

Is our Constitution saying "Say something, I'm giving up on you"??

Dirty Name

When you get angry and swear you call someone a dirty name.

Not nice, but you just have to before, or if, you hit them.

A fight could ensue if you kept it all within and did not do something.

So a dirty name is the sign of uncontrolled emotion and anger.

Say it and you will feel better??

However... however, the receiver of this compliment might be offended and call you one... or even better... take a swing at you.

Politicians call the other party dirty names, though they are more eloquent and oblique. They have their own code language.

Nations do the same when their representatives are interviewed on CNN. We get it. They show restraint, but we know the otherwise. There are nations which foster evil plain and simple. They don't deserve a dirty name. They deserve an economic bomb at the least. Some need a real one dropped from the sky. Have we not learned that violence doesn't respond to aspirin?

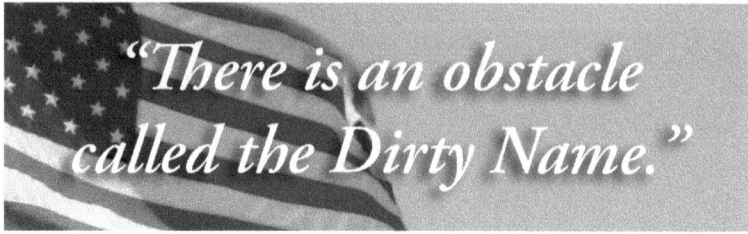

There is an obstacle called the Dirty Name in Coronado California and Little Creek Virginia. It is well known by all Navy SEALs. You look at it and swear. How are you going to attack it? You walk up to it to size it up on your first visit. An instructor explains the goal… to leap to the first log landing on your stomach then the same to the top one. Except they are a little too high. You swear. You call it anything vulgar. It will require total commitment. Big gamble to leap that far and that high. It is an S.O.B.…… You see someone else struggle ahead of you and fall off. Attempt again. Attempt again. Get threatened and humiliated by the instructor. Dig deep and hurl yourself into the unknown and make it.

Life throws curves.

Life is all obstacles if you choose to look at it that way.

So many quit, get depressed, or avoid what is directly in their path.

Seize every moment and overcome with Faith.

Kiss A Cobra

Cobra??

Kiss it??

You nuts??

You mean the snake that stands up with a hood and horrific eyes with a flicking tongue??

Deadly and quick to strike?

Kiss one??

Are you out of your mind?

All too often these days, snakes are hidden behind acronyms. The government and business all have their abbreviations and wording that makes things appear nicer or friendlier than they are.

There is COBRA which is, would you believe, Consolidated Omnibus Budget Reconciliation Act. How many lawyers did it take to put that together? No clue what it involves other than something to do with insurance. Do you want to kiss it?? Be careful. You will get so entangled you will feel strangled.

"I love Customer Service these days."

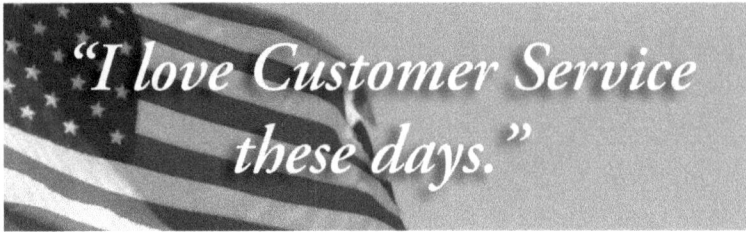

I love Customer Service these days. What a joke with all the voice prompts, bad music, and "we will be with you in just a moment" lies. Or "Press 4 for an Account Specialist", who, by the way is on the phone with her Mom….

Human Resources??? Stay away from them. They are deadly as they record your every word for their database. They have so many legal liability instructions and protocols that you might as well be speaking to a robot. Definitely a Cobra. LOL

The avoidance of direct responsibility is the subtle cancer spreading throughout our entire culture, from child to parent to business to government. All is being protected by "Terms of Agreement". You have to check that small box before you can get anything or go anywhere. Try and read the fine print. Kiss the Cobra.

There was one Cobra that you could kiss and get excited.

Of course, if you over-reacted it could still kill you.

A guy named Carroll Shelby made them for the Ford Motor Company.

It costs a million dollars to kiss a good one today. LOL

He once said, "I woke up one morning and I says 'To h*ll with all this, I'm going to go do what I want to.' " .... As should we.

And he tamed the Cobra so we could enjoy one.

Valuedise Lost

Our nation was founded on core values.

Our first universities had mission statements that all revolved around traditional principles of honesty, truth, integrity, and doing "good".

All came from protesting backgrounds.

They were all Protestants.

They had to fight for their values. They were the cornerstones of this country. Immigrants learned English. We were rich with diversity. In the homes were strict rules.

The United States of America used to be united. Looking at TV today we appear to be the most divided nation on earth. Republicans hate Democrats. Democrats hate Republicans. Atheists hate religions, especially one. A nation of incessant protesting. Minorities now ruling majorities. Go figure???

You are not allowed to discipline a child unless it falls under legal guidelines. LOL.

At the dinner table heads are down into texting cellphones.

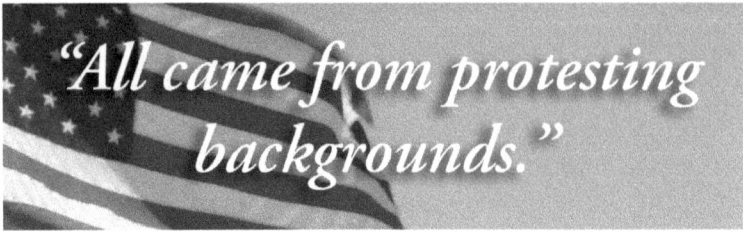

Parents, now single, can't fight the "whatever" attitude that confronts them every moment. The downside of social networking is false ego affirmation that comes from the inherent instant gratification that your friends like you.

Where do kids find values; some ethical or moral compass to go by????

Not looking down.

We used to have Boy Scouts. Parents could say no. Parents could discipline.

Single Moms can't do it all. The family is suffocating. Schools run away from values leadership.

Islam is not allowed criticism. God is.

Churches are mocked. It is not politically correct to acknowledge God inscribed into our municipal buildings and monuments. Upside down??

Paradise Lost. LOL.

It seems to me that the last bastion of order is the military. You are told what you can and cannot do. You learn to respect the flag and country. You learn the value of authority and organization. You learn comradery and trust. You learn about teamwork. I know. Have you been through Hell Week? Ok, I went through it and learned to swear and to talk trash along the way… It's how I survived running 4 miles on a beach in the sleet.

(PS. Walk out of the room now. I believe in the universal draft.)

Let's declare war on the attack on values.

Let's defend our kids and families.

Let's stop our paranoid worrying about the feelings of others and fight for what is "righter".

We are fools if we don't think our Rome will burn.

Let's be value driven and stop all the hogwash infighting.

Let's make it Team America once again.

If not, the new Pearl Harbor and the next 9/11 will bury us.

Valuedise Lost.

Lone Survivor

A mother is standing on a hill grasping the hands of her two small children.

Divorce.

Single parenthood.

A tear unseen.

A choice is weighing down on her soul.

There is a path of short term relief with substances and unnamed people.

But those two pairs of hands...??? To quit or to go forward into the unknown, putting those tiny palms ahead of her own.

We cannot predict the future but we can shape it with each positive, unselfish step. Faith yielding hope. One step at a time.

On a lonely mountain in Afghanistan 4 Navy SEALs chose not to kill a shepherd and a child.

A choice.

You may have read the book or seen the movie. Lone Survivor.

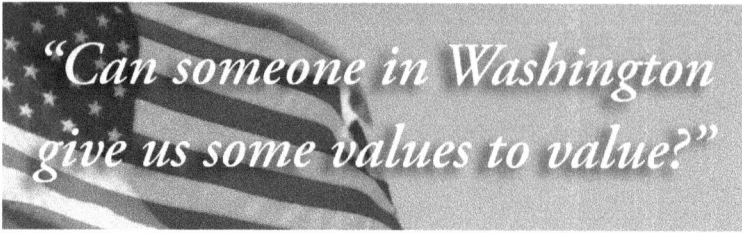

Intense. They became trapped. A young man stood high atop a rock to try to get his satellite phone to transmit his location. He was killed. Mike Murphy fell there forever. His mother left alone on that hill in spirit with him. One Lone Navy SEAL survived. His name is Marcus. He survived to tell the story with grace.

Young women get pregnant.

They no longer know if they will be left on the hill. What has become of us? If a fetus could think would she have second thoughts in this, our celebrated 21st century? Pack it in. Forget it. I don't want to be a burden to my future mother. Save a lot of money on skinny jeans....

What is happening to our men?

The notion of responsibility and commitment appears to have been terminated with prejudice by questionable social forces. Where does a young man go for direction? We have even found a way to neuter the Boy Scouts.

Make mistakes and all you get is sensitivity therapy and assignment of blame to someone or something else.

Where is the man walking back up that hill to take the hands of his woman and children? Is the hill too steep? Is not the reward obvious? Ride up on your four wheeler and load them all on board and get back to being a parent……

Where are the leaders and politicians?

Isn't this the terminal cancer in our society? Roman Empire all over again?

The noise of politicians accusing and complaining is heard all across our nation…. like two parents in the final throws of divorce? The family, the heart of our country will inherit this empty void. This is a bullet at close range.

Forget global warming.

What about the erosion of motherhood and family and values? What do we value any more?

Can someone in Washington give us some values to value?

The Constitution is a good place to look. Why did they bother to write it? And agree? There is also a Book . . .

Mike's mother cried that day.

Her son was cool.

He cared more for others.

He never got to have any children.

He still died for them.

2000 years ago a mother named Mary cried.

Evil

The problem with evil is that we have made a joke out of it.

We have turned our potential and our logic upside down and we don't know it.

Evil has become funny...

That is so funny that the "Riddler" has a field day.

Batman knows. LOL

The only people who know what evil is are those who have tasted it first hand, and seen the reality of real blood, pain, and terror. If you haven't been there then you don't have a clue in your liberated, educated, feelings-driven brain. Not a clue...!

Detached reality is the world we are creating. Radical Islam is in the news, that's all folks. WWI and WWII and Korea and Vietnam and Iraq and Afghanistan did not happen. Even our school history classes ignore how horrible and evil wars were. They won't teach evil. Because by not teaching good they fatally short change us.

Video games make blood just a color... splattered on white walls

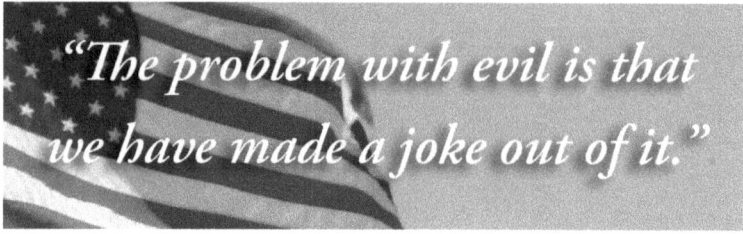

as almost-real brains are blown out. May the good guys win… on their remotes. LOL

Real drones taking real videos from afar of white, human-shaped images, running in the woods that are blown apart with a Hellfire missile. Cheers go up in remote bunkers 3,000 miles away. The evening news excites us with snippets of the audio communications in real time video. Exciting and funny.

Evil is the king of entertainment. Sin is just the icing on the cake. We revel in the mysteries of murder and infidelity. Sex is not sin. It is just feel-good choices. Laws that are problems can be attacked by lawyers… This is all so funny. LOL Triple LOL's!!

AND, then… we have commercials that pay money to finance it all… so we can enjoy looking at sin and evil!! Thank God for the Weather and Hallmark channels… so we can briefly feel better until the next juicy series takes off.

And then,…. We have award ceremonies to honor all those in every form of media for their efforts to make everything entertaining!

We still do have Disneyland and NASA that haven't found a way to insert evil. Stay tuned…

We just have this big problem with the word EVIL. We just won't agree that it exists.

How are our kids going to know how to respect it?

To pass the buck is evil.

Does evil define good...or does good define evil??

Your choice...

Who wins??

I wouldn't bet against evil..............

A Spade

A spade is a spade is a spade.

Doesn't that mean that nothing is no more than what it is??

It doesn't mean that it is a riddle or has other meanings.

It just means that black is black and white is white.

But we can no longer call a spade a spade. Liberals call it one thing and conservatives another. Go figure.

Conservatives say it is a tool that makes entry into a plot of ground and throws the last spadeful on the grave.

Liberals say it is a process of protecting man from having too many pets… and they spell it different. They like neutering everything with academic acclaim.

Therein lies our quandary. And therein lies our defeat in the next war. It is called the "dithering spade" or Grey Tongue Disease, GTD. We debate the obvious and decide nothing. Media gobbles up the disagreement and confusion creates the new grey.

If your fellow citizen is beheaded, I don't think any letter to the NY Times will make a difference. People don't desist from

"But we can no longer call a spade a spade."

bad just because you say it is wrong. They will reconsider their choices if there is real threat of death, economic and mortal. Shoot some first, then ask questions… as the old expression goes.

Why are we so afraid to call a spade a spade? Why have we taken the spades out of our history books? Why are we afraid to use the color black? Why is white now problematic?

Language is becoming vague. Phrases are beginning to mean nothing. We are becoming a nation of insecurities. Afraid to upset anyone. Afraid to be unique. Afraid to have values.

Oh my goodness, what has happened?

Time to gather in small groups with our spades.

And all chant "A spade is a spade is a spade".

Shuffle the deck.

Trump hand?

Reverse Racism

Goes around, comes around...

Slavery. Religion. Wealth. Poverty. Democracy.

Socialism. Communism. Materialism. Informationism.

In our lives we have seen societies stand still, cultures regress, and justice debated ...or some would say deleted...

We killed Martin Luther King. Oops…. Don't go there…..
We, meaning a culture that had not been able to find values universal enough to create barriers to evil and prejudice. We have proceeded down a road where we are making everything that was black or white into our new shade of grey. Laws were established that try to blind one to race rather than embrace it. Subtle, but just as dangerous. Think about it.

Religion has been morphed into an avoidance category. Wealth and poverty are now both evil. Democracy bows her noble knee to lesser.

Socialism and Communism are failures for the people.

Materialism is celebrated as it strips the soul of worth.

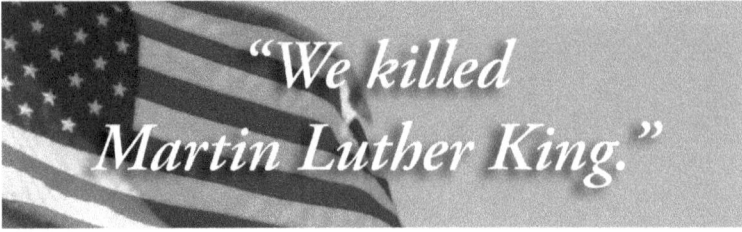
"We killed Martin Luther King."

And lastly, the new "Informationism" is our last hope. With the god of Google we *hopefully* have all the facts. All the facts, past and present!! Truth. Truth sought since Biblical times. Truth at last. Thank God almighty Truth at last....

OK, with media and educators alike having equal access to truth how are we doing??? We have spy satellites and information gathering capabilities beyond imagination. We are all in data mines. You could say our identities are slaves to the data mining industry... Interesting twist?? It's ok with me as I no longer have anything to hide anyway...

Are we better off? Are we doing better??

As we ponder the polls and data of politics we see enormous demographic evolutions in America. Ethnic minorities are becoming the new majorities. People of color are getting their own languages legalized. When was the last time you saw a warranty in English only? Race boxes on forms are increasing. You can't say white... it's Caucasian... Who ever heard of Caucasian?? I am finally insecure about saying white. What do I say? And ... I am becoming the new minority. Goes around comes around....

But *for sure* I am an American, a citizen of the land of immigrants and opportunity. So is it time to take the race check boxes off all forms?? Reverse discrimination is growing. Now that profiling is such a bad process, what are we left with? What can we base judgments on? Better get a lawyer, the new god of truth. Make sure you have been read your "Informationism Rights".

As I write this I wonder where it will all lead. In the best country in the world we have raised disagreement to new heights. Our political parties should be ashamed of not being able to raise the dignity of their process. Self-interest pervades decision making.

I like the most recent quote by someone.

It is "We the People" not "We the Government".

Until we the people refine our common values based on our Judeo-Christian heritage I fear that this white old man will die with a tear on his cheek.

Political Opportunity

Something is confusing me.

Politics is spelled a lot like polite.

Maybe we should rename it.

Wouldn't it be great if a political opportunity became an opportunity to be polite?

Can you imagine a House of Representatives full of seated "politers"? How about a Senate?

We know that everyone on the Supreme Court is polite. Even attorneys are polite in those chambers.

Actually, everyone in church is not polite. They just talk behind backs.... Not to say there is not politics too.

Today politeness is often taken advantage of or disparaged as a weakness. You are told to be strong and forceful. You don't have to be polite with any form or face of evil.

Politeness shows respect. We need to sit down and re-determine what and who we should be polite about or to. Of course, if you

"Politics is spelled a lot like polite."

are a good person, being polite comes naturally. Probably means you had good parents who said "No" a lot... until you got it.

Now there are always opportunities to be polite if you are not lazy. Being polite makes the other person feel good too. And you will probably be closer to an agreement than you would have been otherwise.

Let's make a political opportunity one in which to be nice. Whereas today it is one of criticizing and destroying the opponent.

I am not authorized to use the formal Party names that are donkeys and elephants. You would think they are cowboys running a steel cage match.

Who in the world wants to run for public office? It is more dangerous than ever.

Misinformation is documented and celebrated. Wry political sarcasm trumps honesty and innocence. Comedy is the new serious.

I just don't get those TV shows.

Abused political opportunities are the fertile soil of wars of all sorts.

Eventually reaching beyond our shores.

If we don't start being polite to one another, then there is no God.

All is lost.

Shooting Beauty

What is beautiful about shooting?

Well, sometimes we have to hunt to feed... that goes back 10,000 years.....

Stones, clubs, spears, traps, poison, arrows, bullets, explosives, and whatever else are the tools of killing. Accepted and necessary when they are. It is up to us to determine when and why.

It is all about slowing evil and protecting what one values... That is its own debate. I know what a Glock, Sig Sauer, or a FN P90 is for starters. I own them. I will not leave my family's fate to chance.

Then there are the beautiful things in life, from nature, to children, to all that is pleasing to the eye. Have you not taken a picture of a sunset, or a baby, or a puppy, or a smile that is truly amazing? Shooting pictures is a wonderful way to show what you see and appreciate. Some faces in fashion magazines are so beautiful that they are not real. Or.... a schooner on the ocean against the clouds in full sail. Wonders abound. They are ours to own. Soul food.

"What is beautiful about shooting?"

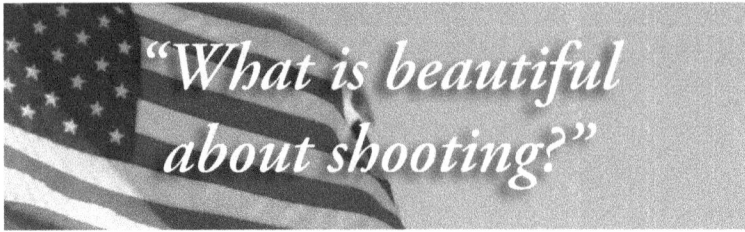

My daughter takes a different view. She made a film called "Shooting Beauty". It is a powerful life-transforming journey into the world of cerebral palsy. It takes courage to watch it but once you have you are better than you were before. I am humbled. Life all too often focuses on the obviously beautiful. How in the world can beauty be found with tragically ostracized beings? Courtney was blessed with a vision to teach these people how to use a camera and take pictures. She fashioned special individualized accessories for them. Each participant learned composition, took pictures…. And… eventually had them on the walls of galleries. Dignity was brought into their lives through photography. You have to see the film. It has won many awards.

You know how we turn our heads when we see someone who is not normal looking? They see you. They see us wincing every day. Hurts. But they understand… *better* than we. You know how people can be made fun of if they are different? You see this film and you become embarrassed at your former behavior as you now know you are causing hurt that you did not intend. Deep inside each of us is a compassion center which is innocent, vulnerable, and sensitive. It is part of our true self. We are not born to hurt. We are born to help. It takes many a lifetime to realize that this is the street of joy. There is no other.

Shooting Beauty should just have begun her journey. Every school in every town should be showing this film. It would stop bullying in its ugly tracks. "You can't say that!" would be the new admonition of a newly energized student majority.

We talk of diversity and sensitivity training.

We talk about our culture's demise.

We talk. We talk.

Beauty lies deep within.

Judge the face and you lose the soul.

Yours.

Minority Rules

We have freedom.

We are a multicultural miracle.

We have an economy powered by democracy with unlimited potential if we get out of the way.

We have taken the spirit of man and created a system where he can grow and gain regardless of his outer shell. In WWII we fought alongside our brothers from the human race, not of a race. Powerful. Ask any veteran of any war. Do you have the courage to actually ask someone who really knows? Or do we lack the courage to so honor them? Think about it. It is so much easier to watch a medal given to someone on TV…. So much easier.

I grew up and we team members voted to see who of us would be captain of the football team. I wasn't voted in. We voted, took a count, and the person getting the majority of the votes won. Majority rules or something. It has worked all through life, for the most part.

We didn't have to deal with the feelings of those who lost, much less mine. It seemed like a fair process. And life went on. Feelings

"We are a multi-cultural miracle."

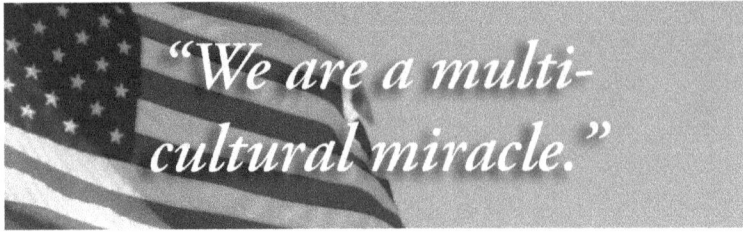

were a natural byproduct of all decisions. Too Bad was okay. Suck it up. Be a man. It worked.

Diversity was and is a blessing. An arrangement of flowers. Human blossoms. Oops, forgot to read the card… "Love God". Except we didn't open the card.

The race of race started with Martin Luther King's tragic murder. The nation shook with grief, anger, and resolve. Movements and laws pounded the establishment and there was no turning back. The problem lay with the majority who had some evolving and maturing to do. It is better now for many. But corruption, greed, and irresponsibility took the wind out of the sails and has left many sitting on the curb. Fatherless homes and jobless masses became the breeding ground for the new poverty. The new prison. And it is diverse. Diversity in crisis.

As the cries of despair rose so did the cries of every injustice. Now something new was going on and that was the emergence of powerful media access to pain. This is good…. But the ensuing (pun intended) search for "who to sue" gave media more material, more news. Pretty soon every minor cause had found a pulpit. The voracious appetite of media for content consumed every local possibility for news. And we fed on it.

The new paradigm became feeling centric. You can't offend

anyone became more important than you can't offend everyone. Repeat it. You can't offend anyone became more important than you can't offend everyone. On any given day a minority news flash became important. Incident after incident… in schools, in homes, at work…… Every wrong became a right with two lawyers in tandem. The majority began to be excluded.

How can a politician cater to so many rights and wrongs, so many causes, without being vilified by even the smallest minority?

Enter the socialist democratic agendas with their infinite sensitivity to the minorities. Rants with ties on. The conservative shrinks. He wishes he were a minority so he would be defended. The majority has become the embattled minority.

But I still have faith in our God-given potential to revere good, selflessness, and compassion.

I still believe the American dream of old where a handshake was a million times more efficient than fine print.

Back then the minority ruled as each individual contract had value.

Our minorities deserve the same.

Instructor Waddell

I wrote a piece a while ago entitled DTMWTD…. Don't tell me what to do.

It was targeted at kids who don't like their parents telling them what to do…

Well… and maybe husbands too??? You get the picture… any of us at any time. DTMWTD.

When we tell someone what to do we are trying to warn them of possible consequences that we see that we think they don't?

We all have to learn the same hard way by experiencing and dealing with our own decisions. We want them to be ours. Why should we trust anyone else's opinion? "Enough with the advice" we say. Of course, I am still saying that to my wife today….

Then… when we get a job we have to listen to our boss. *Groan.* If we really grow up we listen to our customers and clients, not ourselves. This is difficult, but it happens as it is paycheck driven. We listen and learn.

So it appears it is the *incentive* that is important. What is the incentive today when all kids withdraw into the self-assuring

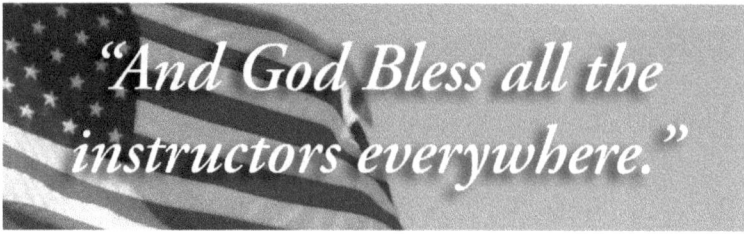

"And God Bless all the instructors everywhere."

world of their cell phone? We are in trouble. They are affirmed by their insecure social network, not by our wisdom. They no longer "look up" to anything.

The word "No" is not allowed. Children are taught the nuances of "child abuse" and only have to tell their teachers and there will be a knock on the door.

I was blessed with great parents, spankings, and a plethora of "No's". Thank God.

But it was not until the military did I fully begin to appreciate what "No" meant. If you wanted to be a Navy Frogman/ SEAL the INSTRUCTORS were waiting with snarling teeth and monstrous threats of pain. If you did not say "YES INSTRUCTOR" to everything they suggested there was a real price. Too many pushups, too many sit-ups, too many pull-ups, too many runs, too many swims... "Are they crazy?" I would think to myself. Is this nonsense really worth it? Why were they so strict?

Why was Instructor Bernie Waddell so scary behind his wry smile?

Why??? Because all hell could rain down on you if you showed disrespect in any way, shape, or form. So just do what he asked and get on with your moment. Mile after mile crawling, running, and swimming in the freezing winter during Hell Week weeded out the survivors. The Yes Men.

You see... the instructors knew what would happen to you if you were not forged properly. You would be killed when it could have been avoided. Your swim buddy would have been put in peril unnecessarily. The mission aborted because you did not heed your instructor.

We need instructors to become all that we have the potential to become. Values must be honed in sweat and pain. We need to learn that freedom is not for free. If you are not conditioned you will not be strong enough to stand in the winds of life. Laziness destroys potential.

There is white and black, good and evil, yes and no, do's and don'ts.....

Values became valuable.

Serving others became more important than serving self.

Prayer became real.

Morality was affirmed.

God Bless You Instructor Bernie Waddell... and Godspeed.

And God Bless all the instructors everywhere.

And parents too.

Shameless

Shameless the way some people behave.

You just want to look away sometimes.

But maybe we are looking away more and more today.

Shameless.

The headlines reek of inevitable war. Of unspeakable acts going on every day. I don't get it? Why do people still hold human life as so inconsequential? Is it centuries of poverty and lack of leadership? Is a religion all that gives hope?

Is not atrocity unacceptable? Women and even children? Hello world?

Text bombs don't appear to be stopping anything but good.

Shameful.

At what point or border do our brothers cease being our brothers?

What if we didn't fund Special Operations? Those guys go where none of us wishes to go. They get sent because it means fewer

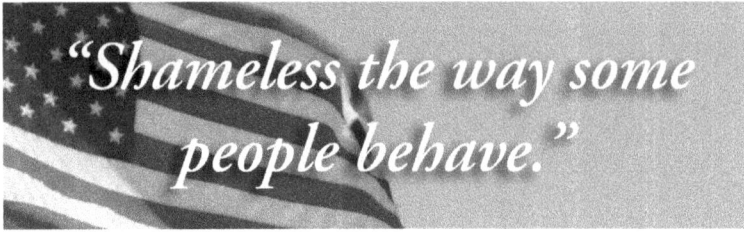

lives to risk rather than the thousands with the forces actually required. We pat them on the back and have no clue what they do. Do for us, that is. Shameful.

They can only be successful in cloaks of total secrecy. We are doing our best to take that away from them. Shameful. Shameless.

Evil so sublime is also infiltrating our culture. It seems like we are being called to sameness. Every special interest is claiming foul and unfairness so law after law is being enacted. The majority is becoming overwhelmed by the minority's claims.

See the parallel between the Middle East and our "Shames"? We are fighting politically to all have the same opinions. Are we beheading values? Law after law calling us to act and think the same. Really good people are afraid to speak up for fear of being drowned out by the placard people.

Do we want to allow ourselves to be more or less the same? Look-a-Likes?

Maybe we need some moral SEALs to take on the fight when they are discharged.

Who else can we turn to?

Rules

Rules are meant to create order and keep one from harm.

Rules try to put us on a path that ends in good......

Well, it so happens that we did not like the original rules.

Guess what? We then wrote more rules to make the original rules easier to manage. Okay... Our legal system seemed fine and things hummed along...

Then what the heck happened?

This country was founded on principles which now have come to be out of date??

Go figure??

Were our founding fathers just not sensitive enough?

Of course, they could have had no vision as to the impact of new technologies. Do we still hold their principles to be transcendent and based on the sanctity and worth of the individual? Lofty goals? (Pun intended.)

Now I remain positive about our potential to strive for higher goals. (Last pun intended).

"Rules try to put us on a path that ends in good..."

But do we not get it?... That more rules and regulations inevitably complicate this journey?

Legislators have become the minions of legal technicality. Lawyers are so prolific that they are like waiters in a legal soup kitchen... Lawyers have these ear trumpets tuned to the sound of anyone in disagreement, waiting to issue volumes of self-justification.

Then again, lawyers are our paperwork police. Heroes in a complex world where their long hours looking for truth is a service to all.

As long as they are serving us.

As long as their principles are lofty and unselfish....

"In order to proceed, click on agree".

Which we do as the fine print associated would require us to have a lawyer. How absurd that they cover their fannies while we can't afford to.... CYA is now a driving legal force in every enterprise. Ever try to read the fine print? It is a waste of time.

Did you try to read the ballot on Election Day?

It was an insult to the voter.

Disrespectful in its incoherency.

Rules are now so confusing that they are creating disorder and harm.

This is not where we began.

Glass Ceiling

A glass ceiling seems to me to be something nobody wants in their home.

Can you imagine looking up and seeing the mess the kids are making?

What about looking up and seeing Mom and Dad chasing each other in their pajamas?

There are just things that do not need to be seen.

Or how about being able to look down and see what your staff is doing? Or what is on their screens. Or what they just wrote about you on a sticky note they were passing around.

Glass ceilings would let you see more bad things than you needed I fear.

Why is it that we want to know everything about everybody? We have the scandal magazines, fostering a slew of millionaire paparazzi. Professionals who know how to see behind everything. Well…. Maybe they keep us honest??

Our big problem with what we see is that we tend to distort it

"Now we have a problem with women."

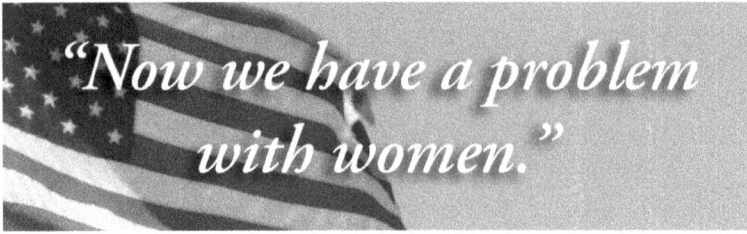

with our own bias; our own lens. Truth becomes ever so slightly changed. And the next person adds their own spin.

So maybe a glass ceiling lures us with its transparency. Be nice to have all over Washington?? Everybody being able to see everything except Top Secret. That's what they promise when campaigning. What happened?

It is most often the invisible that stops progress that nullifies Truth. Whispers and gossip eat away at substance. Hmmm? Get it?

Now we have a problem with women.

They want equal rights.

They want to have those heavy emergency window breakers in their handbags. So whenever they come up against a glass ceiling, they can "slam, bam, thank you mam" break the door down. Shatter the obstacles. They don't cost much.

But then again neither does keeping a campaign promise….

Wouldn't it be great if all HR, Human Resources, (what a contrived name), interviewers gave out a free Window Breaker Emergency Escape Tool as a sign of their commitment to transparency?

Fairness lies out there if we turn inward to our conscious.

A deal can be struck with women for women.

Who's first?

Let's get the job done.

The Decision

Life isn't fair.

Some are lucky and some are not.

Some are born in the United States and some are born in Africa.

Some are born into Christianity and some are born into Islam.

Some live their lives in Nike's and some in bare feet.

Some should be glad and some should be angry. Some have iPads and some have nothing. Some travel and some go nowhere. Some are rich and some are poor. Why are there slums?

We send our sons to fight wars to protect our shores. It has to be done … or you have your head in the sand or in your social network looking down. In the military these sons bond intensely in ways we do not know. It is the finest of wines. It is idealism in the raw. When a life is lost it is like a baby being ripped from a womb. Multiple combat tours with the same unit forges courage and knowledge in an intimacy foreign to most. Living the extremes of trust.

IED's (Improvised Explosive Devices) have made it all the more

absurd and difficult for the participants. Lost limbs and lives in an instant. The victim who lives is almost worse off. Sent home. No more responsibility for his buddies. A nightmare of pretense and bad dreams lies ahead.

Veterans don't talk about what they saw as we would not understand … much less appreciate. So the silent prison forms. Peers are no longer that. Jobs are very difficult to find. The new combat is with the bureaucracies. Self is lost in the mountain of forms and databases. No one hires. Interviews fewer and less comfortable. Pride diminished. A life feels lost.

Why are veteran suicides greater than combat deaths?

There should be a quota for all businesses to hire veterans.

They put it all on the line for us.

Why can't we do that for them?

Let's take their tragic decision away from them.

The Drill Instructor

The Drill Instructor (DI) barks out his commands to the frightened cadre.

"Gimme 50!!!"

"Backs straight!!"

"Chest must touch the ground!!"

"Full extension!!"

"Get that back straight! How many times do I have to tell you??!!"

"OK, stay at lean and rest until I come back, children!"

Do you think they make Marines, soldiers, much less Navy SEALs by asking them what they would prefer to do? Do you think the Drill Instructors have graduated from sensitivity training? Are Democratic Constitutional rights in effect? Are the recruits entitled?

I postulate that this just must might be about life and death, not feelings. I think this may be about protecting your freedoms and your right to complain. But this cannot happen without young men prepared for battle and for death.

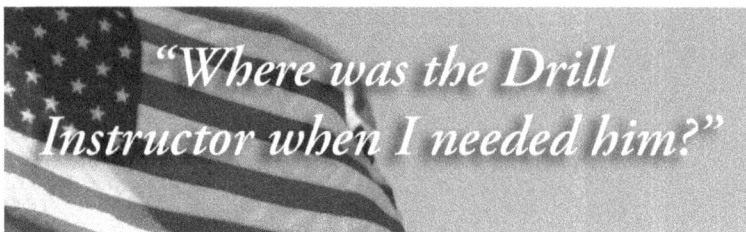

"Where was the Drill Instructor when I needed him?"

Huuuhhh??? Hello?? You have got to be kidding! OMG you can't be serious! Death doesn't happen other than on the news and usually far away. Whatever. Text me later… I am busy.

I am of the opinion that every young able bodied male should drafted. Boys become men much sooner than on the playing fields or the streets.

We sure don't like systems which tell us what to do. It is like it is in our DNA to rebel against authority. Go away Dad, go away teacher, go away policeman, go away boss, go away reality. I am armored with my self-serving iPhone and the courage of my social network.

We allow the Drill Instructors of life to make us miserable as long as it keeps us from getting killed. We love our bodies as they are our ego cathedrals.

But what about the Drill Instructor in the clouds? He wants to save our souls and enrich our lives beyond our wildest imagination. Problem is… We don't have any imagination.

How many individuals choose paths right into the combat zones of greed, lust, envy, pride, gluttony, anger, and filth? Drugs, alcohol, sex, vanity, indifference, and jealousy and…on and on.

"Well, I didn't think it would be this bad. A little more won't hurt…"

Consciences trampled by disdain for authority and logic.

Where is the Drill Instructor when I needed him? Everyone doesn't screw up their lives. I see some happy people around… No not the hypocrites… just a lot of normal people going about their business, helping others, and laughing. How do I become one of them?

Well, duuuhhh??

Hello?

The Drill Instructor is in the sky!

No pain no gain they always said….

American Sniper

American Sniper is a movie made from a book by a real person.

It is biographical non-fiction.

The author was murdered.

Chris Kyle was a good man.

A very good man.

His murderer was sick and evil and one of us.

This movie is on the way to be one of the all-time largest grossing films. All competition are fantasy fiction movies. All the rest are pure entertainment and escapes from reality.

American Sniper is not. Its greatness and appeal is from confronting issues head on with artistic realism. We are forced into conversations that all other movies avoid. What to do about evil? Who can do something about it? Does evil exist? We get criticized if we try to define what is good or bad. Sad state of affairs.

The movie makes us think about what military families give up for us. The movie provides moral dilemmas facing the soldier.

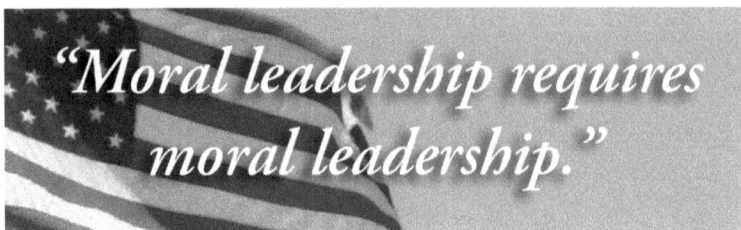

It is not impersonal but personal. Memories haunted by acts of horror and doubt.

We have Navy SEALs to do some special assignments in the quiet. Risk taking at the extreme. Beyond conventional boundaries. Special Warfare is special. Training is beyond imagination. You know nothing about it.

The movie misses giving us a real feeling of the exhaustion and pain endured.

Hell week is a week of indescribable fortitude and compromise. You have to give up your being to trust. Trust that you will not die. You may quit at any time. A choice that terrifies you every moment.

Leaders are forged.

They know what it takes.

Moral leadership requires moral leadership.

The world needs us.

"Quitting is not an option."

The Greatest Democrat

The greatest Democrat has yet to be born or yet to claim the throne.

It is within reach.

The greatest Democrat must simplify codes and vision.

Values must be reclaimed in clarity.

The deserving poor must be embraced, not dehumanized by bureaucracy. Those who work hard must be lauded, those who do not must accept responsibility not a handout.

Fairness comes from ethics and morals.

A great Democrat cannot parse values.

He must stand for truth, compassion, and accountability.

Lastly, and most difficult is to bring all together under a common vision of unity not division. Class and demographic distinction, aka warfare, must be targeted as corrosive and deadly.

I could go on, but you get the picture.

In fact, you should take up the lead.

> *"The greatest Democrat should be the greatest Republican."*

In fact, the greatest Democrat should be the greatest Republican, or vice versa.

In fact, neither will survive if they don't take off their red and blue ball caps and act like an all-star team against the perils ahead.

Lincoln

I just saw "Lincoln".

I just saw our Lincoln for the first time not in marble.

I just saw our nation born in values by a man assassinated.

This brooding film, mostly about conversation and perseverance, is disturbing and unfamiliar in its darkness and lack of action. Yet, it is a newborn masterpiece that brings us into a man of deep character who refused to be stuck in the mud of racism.

You leave the theatre thanking God that Lincoln lived just long enough to get the vote passed. What would our nation be for the Negro had Lincoln caved in to the enormous political storm at the ending of the Civil War?

Equality at last for the slave. Absolutely unheard of. Yet here we are still with its vestiges and sensitivities. White and black alike are carving out colorless relationships. I have seen much of the good, but know that lingering pains lie beneath surfaces.

Subtle vestiges of racial snobbery and stereotype continue to exist. The entitlement cancer hurts one more than the other. The drug decimation of the parent and family has insured racial discord as the fatherless child is reared in less than acceptable conditions.

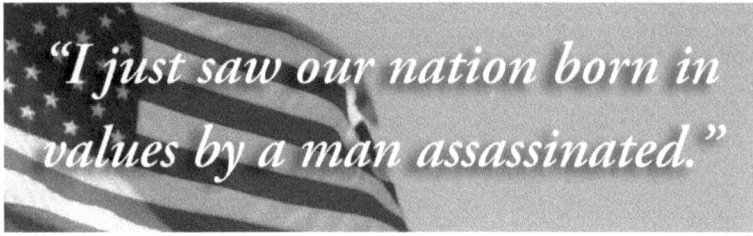
"I just saw our nation born in values by a man assassinated."

Why are we so naive to think we can legislate the lack of love away?

Who chucked proven values out the window?

Who liberated the liberal from his liberal forefather's commitment to rights? Genius move I must say. Conservatives are liberals. They too want what is good for all.

It is like a guilty conscience governs prudence rather than commitment to beliefs.

We are lost again.

"Four score and seven years ago our fathers brought forth on this continent a new nation conceived in liberty and dedicated to the proposition that all men are created equal."

The Gettysburg Address as prefaced by Abraham Lincoln.

Equality and clarity period.

What more do we need in Washington?

Let's send our Navy SEALs there to rescue us from ourselves.

Hillary for President

Hillary for President.

OK… I had to use this title to get you to read this…

Yep, I tricked you… but did I?

What are the requirements to be a good leader? Does it hold for both business and politics? How about educators, scientists, humanitarians?? Do we have different standards for different leaders, executives, officers????

Well, I bet that today they have to be insensitive…have no feelings… that's what I think. For if they show feelings the media will be all over them.

Criticism is in vogue and is the fast-info food of the masses. Masses?? That's you and me. Scour backgrounds for anything. Vilify and roast at 6:30 PM. If one has a human tic or uniqueness see if you can make fun of it or SNL it…. Where is class? Where is respect? Who is responsible for what? Is there anything we won't text???

How much fun is it to be a President and be continuously mocked by the opposition? Mocked? Mocked almost sounds Biblical.

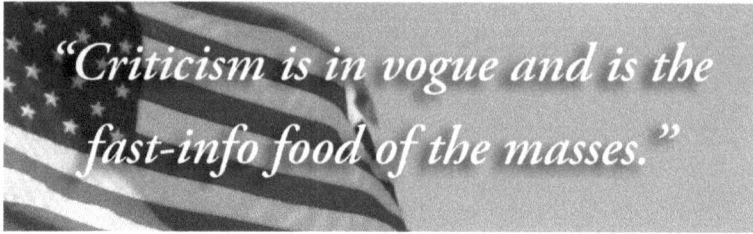

"Criticism is in vogue and is the fast-info food of the masses."

If you listened to the mocking you would think that every President has been a buffoon. Has anyone sat in their skins? Has anyone listened to all the expert advice they have been offered by those surrounding them, the media, and anyone who can reach them? Hindsight for us makes it easy to mock mercilessly with chosen perspective and bias meant to drive home the still elusive truth.

Were we in the oval office when one man had to make a decision to which there was no assurance? Hawk or dove….we won't know for a 100 years. Invade? Drop the atomic bomb? Increase sanctions? What do we really know in our lifetimes???

Ok… We have established you had better not have feelings.

Now, most important is that you must have experience, and lots of it. I would hope you have governed, run a business, held office, and had developed communication skills. Without all these you are in trouble. Good luck. History will not be kind to the novice. Let's make the Presidency PG-60.

As they say in real estate….. Location, location, location. As we should say in the oval office….. Integrity, integrity, integrity. Character defines every moment. A past can have its spots but can also be a powerful sculptor of character.

Hide nothing and win everything.

In fact who can throw the first stone?

And why do we act like we can???

Hillary is running.

Who can run against her with class?

The Camaraderie

It is the camaraderie.

One searches for truth and meaning under the guise of what makes one feel good.

There is entertainment, friendships, and all kinds of things which appear to be what life is.

Often these are devoid of purpose, just activities that make one feel good in the moment.

But why I am here echoes deep within. Where do I make a difference? This is the man-quest. Women have birth and family. Man searches. Man succumbs to aloneness and journeys that lead nowhere. There is pain without purpose.

Military veterans come home and bring their private pain and surface smiles. Many have seen the belly of the beast. But it is the basic training and living together as brothers with tomorrow's uncertainties that forges a bond unimagined by civilians, by families even....
Eating and sleeping often in extremely difficult circumstances. Never knowing the closeness of the unseen enemy or trap. There is always a mission and purpose to the next day... if it is just to take care and be with your buddies, your brothers in camouflage.

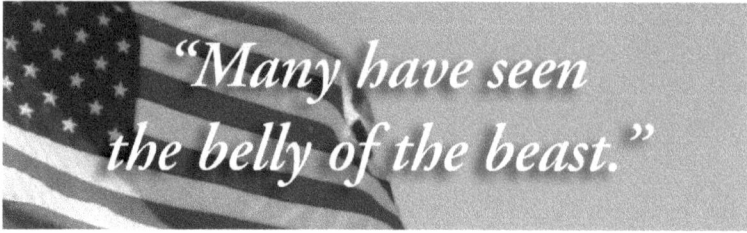

> *"Many have seen the belly of the beast."*

The meaning of your life is defined and private prides are worn.

Then you embark from the returning aircraft and receive the hugs of family. No one knows what your eyes have seen. They want you back as before. You are not the same. They can't get it....only your buddies who are spread far and wide from states to cemeteries.

Finding a job is often hard. Employers have no shared experience. They have no clue as to the disciplines and focus you have experienced. They are the amateurs in life, but don't know it. You have graduated, but don't know it.

Manhood comes from the camaraderie of combat; of getting close to evil. From being next to a buddy's last breath. From touching an artificial limb.

One had learned to communicate without sound. Eye contact rules...

Caring for a buddy more than one's self.

It's the damned camaraderie stupid.

Hire a veteran.

You owe it to yourself.

DDG 112 Hooyah

When something bad happens we all stop our moment and react.

Like when the earthquake was felt this week.

My wife and her girlfriends got scared and confused.

Natural.

But when I talked with my buddies their immediate reaction was as mine… "What do I do right now?". "Who needs to be protected and how?" That is ok, that is the way life has been created. Nurture or protect, our primal roles.

Some things are meant to be natural, left alone…..as they are part of nature, our nature. We are born. We die. This is natural. This is accepted. We can leave it alone or we can try to alter. Man can dignify it or man can desecrate it. Good or evil. Selflessness or selfishness.

People's lives can pay tribute to life or they can cheapify it… (New word, cheapify, or cheapen… I like cheapify…) Hitler made life cheap. Our soldiers ennobled it. Love makes life beautiful. Addictions make life ugly.

"Mike took his final bullets standing."

When something bad happens something has to be done about it. "Done" does not mean debate! "Done" does not mean politicize. Nike says "Just do it". So do I. Attack fast; don't dither it. Inaction is the very worst form of action.

We have a military because history has taught some of us that bad things have and do happen.

Diplomacy works often but not always.

There are people who lie no matter how much we give and try to understand. We may even have to act without anyone else's permission. While all the public posturing is going on, there is not a day when someone in the military is not somewhere operating covertly, much less an innocent drone hovering for the next "perfect" kill. Our Special Operations and Intelligence communities have their lives on the line daily to allow us the delicacy of thinking peace is at hand; that we are safe.

If something goes bad…. Our good guys are sent to situations you would cringe at, or withdraw into psychosis over.

DDG 112 USS Michael Murphy was commissioned and launched in NYC. I was honored to be at the christening in Maine the year prior. I knew Mike at the start of his journey. Many of you may have read the book "Lone Survivor". Mike was a SEAL officer who was sent really deep into the bad. On a lonely mountain in Afghanistan he and 2 of his men were killed by the Taliban. One miraculously escaped and live to tell the story. Mike took his final bullets standing with his radio so he could get clear transmission.

What one does for others is the measure of one's life. You can take bullets on a hill or you can take criticism in your home. It does not matter as long as you are standing up for good. Calling a spade a spade... calling bad for what it is, period.

We have become passive in our beliefs.

We have become afraid to say out loud what we really feel, what our heart tells us.

We don't listen to our heart because it may be politically incorrect.

Proactive or passive about life?

About values?

About evil?

At the end of the ship's commissioning ceremony on the Hudson River a yell by the 1,000 people there of "HOOYAH MIKE!" resonated in the piers and hearts nearby.

When I was told this, my stomach turned and my heart became so heavy...and tears flowed because the word "Hooyah" is so unique to a very special community in Naval Special Warfare to which I once belonged.

Godspeed & Hooyah Mike.

Forever Silent

What do we know about what we don't know about?

How can we judge when we don't know the whole Truth?

But we do judge, and fervently claim we are right.

Do we have heroes we never know about?

The submariner's Silent Service?

The CIA operative?

The Green Beret alone out there?

The Stealth flight that never existed?

The SEAL returning unseen?

The private pain of a veteran?

The tear of a wife?

Heroes in humility.

Keeping us free.

Allowing us to smile.

"Do we have heroes we never know about?"

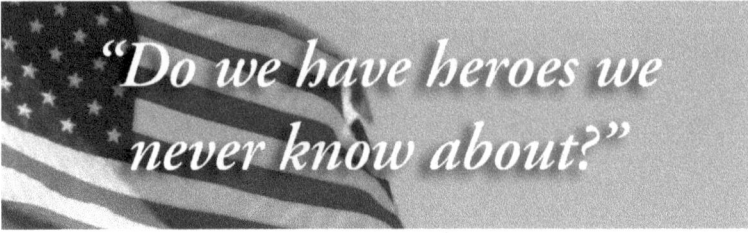

Who pins the medals on them?

We will never know.

They want it that way.

God Bless America.

Entitled

Now this is going to be the most difficult chapter to write and the most difficult to understand.

You are entitled to a full explanation of what is due to you.

You should never accept anything less than the truth.

That is your right.

From your parents came the decision to gamble with your existence and after that magical moment you were entitled to your first breath. No one has a right to take that away from you. Tell me if that is what you think. But more importantly are you entitled to love?? I think so. What is the point of life if you aren't entitled to love? Think about it. You have to make some decisions at some time in your life. Think about it.

What has value and what does not? I think we think we are entitled to value. Well, we get to make choices on what to buy based on value. We are entitled to that right. The right to purchase what we want, when we want… right? We are entitled to love when we want? Right? Are we entitled to good behavior on the part of others??? Are others entitled for us to act responsibly and with compassion? A lot to think about.

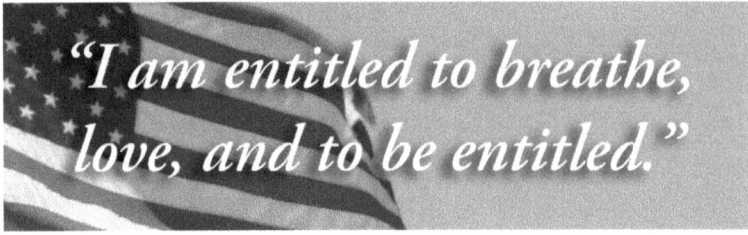

Are bad guys entitled to justice? Are nice Democrats and nice Republicans entitled to a country safe from harm and debt? If I am rich am I entitled to respect? If I am poor am I entitled to respect and compassion? If my neighborhood has been invaded by crack dealers am I entitled to a way out? Maybe.....

Years ago, before you were born, the concept of entitlement was seldom heard as everyone was so busy working and helping one another. Hands were held and hope was the force that launched our amazing nation. Immigrants from England, Ireland, France, Italy, and Spain came on boats of all sorts. Nothing like today. Conditions were marginal to say the least. Ellis Island was full of our fathers looking like deer in the headlights. They expected nothing. The only thing they felt entitled to was freedom from discrimination. That is what the United States offered to those wishing to gamble their pasts and plights. Only hope. Entitled to hope.

WWI and WWII were fought as we felt we were entitled to freedom. Look at every cemetery from Normandy to Arlington. Seas of white freedom crosses. They were entitled to their crosses. They are entitled to our prayers and gratitude.

Whatever happened to our great country? Yes, there has been selfishness and greed and crime that created the need for more laws. Laws require millions of people to obey and as many to interpret and enforce. Bureaucracies of enforcement and code grew under the radar screen. Paperwork justifying paperwork became a cancer. Insurances that insured everything metastasized. Groups of interest unified and these unions became monoliths where members now became managed rather than served. Somewhere entitlement became the vision of this new culture. Be lucky enough to work for a public bureaucracy and you have pensions and insurances second to none. Special interests protecting special interests. The politics of survival has become entitlement.

In this new world order of entitlement our young are just expecting more. Our culture is of instant gratification. Media, video, headphones, and the iPhone have become the Pavlovian conditioning elements of entitlement. With jobs scarce and debt responsibilities ignored at both the personal and national level, chaos is near.

Kids expect money.

The next generation expects to be paid more for less.

We oblige and nurture the "entitled"....

While they text one another...

I am entitled to breathe, love, and to be entitled.

If so, then the end is near.

Something Fishy

Sometimes something just feels not right.

Premonition?

Or just a private suspicion that something is fishy....

Feel that way about the world?

There is so much poverty and violence and it is now the 21st century! We have put man on the moon and an apple on our wrist. What gives?

Why in the USA are there so many poor? We can understand Africa and the Middle East... but the USA?

Admittedly we have been nourishing an entitlement subculture, but there is more to it than that.

The rich are getting richer they say... Our financial institutions have fees on transactions that insure most walk away with less. Why does a hedge fund manager or even a broker get paid so much for phone calls promoting us gambling on "sure" things? The art of the deal?

Workers still provide the product and seldom share in these

profits. Something is fishy. We are a nation, a democracy that is a family of the Constitution of fairness and justice. The rich really can afford to do with less. They would still be creative and productive with half their incomes.

There are companies that truly respect the employee and really take care of them. Unions aren't needed when there is honesty and true appreciation of the contribution every employee makes.

We have tiered ourselves into inefficient structured bureaucracies where supervisor reports to supervisor who reports to supervisor. Fertile ground for politics??

How often does the CEO go into his trenches and shake the hands of the supervised?

Who praises whom and how... and when??

In WWII factories sprang up all across the nation to produce war materials; 500 bombers a day. And we felt good. And most everyone had an honest job.

There was no money being skimmed by financial fishermen....

Values were different then. That war had to be won. We are the beneficiaries. Yet we have also enabled the next war by not keeping our values intact. Values in the boardroom and values in the home.

Have we created the greatest Ponzi scheme of them all?

Pretending we are found when we are lost?

Something is fishy.

I sure love the Swan River Fish Restaurant across the street.

Eyes

The "I's" have it… or the "Aye's" have it.

Or the "Eyes" have it.

Well, then?? Who has it?

Who has the Truth??

I want to see it with my own eyes. Then I will believe it. Then I will know what the Truth is. But sometimes… yes, sometimes you don't get to see it with your own eyes.

The first assertion… The "I's" have it is really interesting. People tell us they believe it or they saw it and we are to believe them. This is based on their "I". Their person. Their ego?? How many times do we rely on the "I" of another person to validate something? The witness of someone else to be the definer of Truth. We then are relying on another "I" to be honest. Interesting. .. But what about only trusting what you see with your own "eyes"???

The nautical nature of "Aye, Aye, Sir!" brings up another notion in this sea of life and Truth we are exploring. "Aye, Aye" means Yes, I will do as directed. There is a truth in that. In the US

"I want to see it with my own eyes."

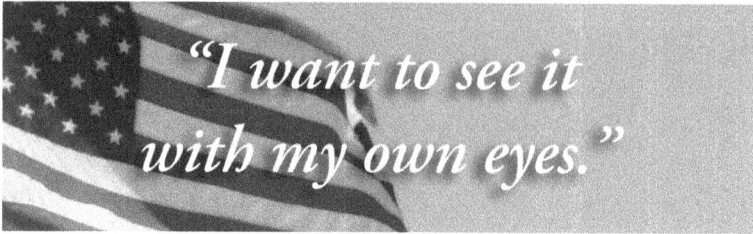

Senate you vote "Aye" or "Nay", yes or no. Something passes when the "Aye's Have It". Something becomes law.

Right now we have this absurd impasse with debt and direction. A lot of "I's" have to say "Aye" for clarity to emerge and we can see with our own "Eyes" what our future looks like. But we have to first agree upon values for an "Aye" to be relevant to Truth and our survival.

We are stripping our walls of our first beliefs.

We don't know where to look anymore to find unison.

Today pot is praised and cigarettes are banished.

The family is legal fodder.

Entitlement abuse is destroying initiative.

The "Aye's" have proclaimed the "I's" the victor.

I am seeing it with my own eyes.

No Buds

Today is Memorial Day 2015.

I took a half hour walk this morning.

I used to run, but heart surgery has changed my lifestyle.

I have run thousands of miles in my lifetime.

From Europe to China. The first plane into Beijing and Shanghai after normalization in 1975. Runs done in smoke, cold, and fog… Alone for miles. No one would look up. They were scared of westerners and didn't want to get in trouble.

The sounds of the people at exercise or work was its own symphony. All around the world. Birds. Running was a journey into the vibrancy of the unknown.

Real entertainment. Not a reality show.

Recently I have been trying out some wireless earbuds. I have noticed all the young wearing them all the time, be it for phone or music. Exercise machines are driven by their drivers who are lost in the music. The outside world is irrelevant. The sounds of the world around are put in their proper place, the background.

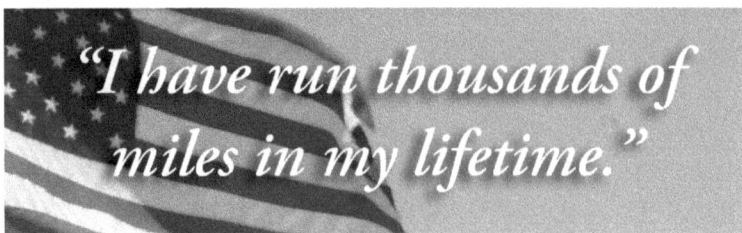

These buds are the seeds of pleasure and deceit. The Truth of the moment is obscured by the allure of good music. Reality controlled. The pain of exercise is muted in the distractions of the top 10.

Our world is upside down. It is becoming more and more difficult to deal with our political indecision and with the evil brewing elsewhere.... Certainly in the Middle-East...

A choice is imminent. Tune out... or tune in. Remove the ear buds if you want a shot at surviving.

There are no earbuds at the Navy SEAL BUD/S (Basic Underwater Demolition/SEAL training).

The harsh reality of unrelenting excessive physical exercise and meaningless repetitions of pain are without the soothing music in the ear... LOL....

If you want to survive and get the prize then your new tunes are the drill instructor's incessant shouts of criticism. Real music in real time. Molding real musicians with new real instruments, those of war... and our survival.

Why don't we get it?

We argue, criticize, and litigate with so much energy that we are mentally exhausted.

If we don't take the damn things out of our ears there will be no home to come home to.

Why don't we get it?

If we can't hear the Truth…

It will be too late.

No buds at BUD/S.

Get it?

Born Into

Wait a second.

Wait...

Hold all that opinion and judgment.

Shoes are made for walking.

Whose shoes have you walked in?

When you were born, where was it? California, Uganda, Damascus, Port-au-Prince, or Pyongyang? How come I was born in New York? Sure glad I was not born in all those other places where discomfort and injustice is the rule. Do we ever really count our blessings before we judge all those souls fighting misery and corruption every hour of every day?

Don't get me wrong... right is not wrong...and wrong is not right. Meaning evil is not good...

You get to choose how to lead your life.... You get to choose what is of value. But where you were born, through zero choice of your own, makes chances to lead a good life a toss-up. If you live in a third world country your media access is a joke...or certainly the

"How do I know what you were born into?"

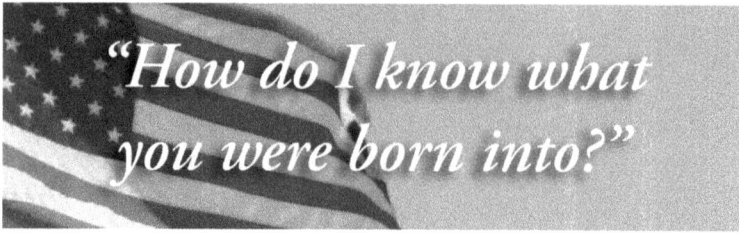

quality of it. Your freedom from want ... both physical and mental is marginal. How do you avoid bad political teachings? How do you avoid the cancers of falsehood and corruption? How do you even know what you were born into?

Were you born into a bad country, a bad family, a bad economy, a bad location, a bad time? Or good ones?

Isn't it funny (not) that we tend to judge others as if they thought like we did and understood walking in our shoes? If I care about you, I assume you care about me. If you "friend" me in Facebook are you really a friend?

How do I know what you were born into?

How do we trust? It is getting less and less easy to trust. Why?

Funny...our American soldiers in Afghanistan trust each other. Why?

Once upon a time we were all born into the same values. A handshake was trusted. Your word was trusted.

What has happened?

What have we abandoned to get us here?

We now have to trust the indecipherable fine print.

We have to trust that government will protect us.

What are our children being born into?

Debt or Prison

A trillion dollars of debt!

Now that is a figure I can work with.

I can get my arms and brain wrapped around that one.

Multiples of a trillion are now easier to manage.

A trillion dollars, yessss.

Debt is always something you want to reduce to zero. I am told the happiest people are the ones with no debt and who do not spend beyond their income. Those are the crazies out there who quietly manage and enjoy life. They never feel they are owed anything. Where in the world did they get such a misdirected notion?? Where??

Now back to the trillion. Just a thousand billion dollars. Let's see… if I give half of my $50,000 income to pay down my personal debt of a trillion dollars I will be able to borrow again in 400 million years. Ok, I up the payment to $250,000 a year and it will only take 4 million years. Ok, so we get 400 million people to pay 25K per trillion dollars of debt and…??? It's all in the math. Hmmm, a trillion is bigger than I thought. I think none of us has

> **"Debt is always something you want to reduce to zero."**

any idea how large it really is… I don't think the government does either.

Okay, math does not work. There is no logic to it. Let's pay it off in 10 years. A 100 billion a year will do it; not including interest, of course.

Now when I get in debt at the mini household level and my credit cards max out I am in trouble. No more discretionary buying, or should I call it "indiscretionary" buying?? No more going out. No more vacations. The predicament is very painful and embarrassing. I can't go out and have my card declined in public. Bad. How to escape the embarrassment. Drinking? With less money and cash?? I don't think so. Without my credit card I am nobody.

Debt used to be so fun. I was always able to stay ahead of it. Thought the government…. Thought the government……

Future generations are at risk… but that is the future…. not now. But wait, these are my kids and grandkids. My excess has put bullseyes on their foreheads.

Their dollar will be worth much less.

Bet a Big Mac will be $20.00.

That is prison. …..

Debt or Prison?

Debtor's prison….

RWE

Romeo Whiskey Echo.

Are we happy?

Are we having a good time?

Are we making a difference?

Or are we just worrying about self?

Are we fighting any battle that means something?

Are we trying to help stop the arguing?

Who would have thought that the letters RWE could pose so many questions? They almost ask us if we ask ourselves enough questions. What about our youth? Are they being asked the right questions? And more important, are they being held accountable for their answers?? Or their actions?

Are there enough laws to insure that all actions are correct? And to what end? Laws used to be about what is good. Now they are drifting towards the political correctness of feelings. Fairness only exists when feelings are not hurt. The new paradigm.

"Are we happy?"

With our political system looking like chaos to the rest of the world, we are no longer presenting the democratic model of efficiency and rightness. Right used to be what is good. We all used to agree on what was good. There was the right way and the wrong way, and children were taught it. History was without bias. Religion was respected.

Are we ignoring evil? It seems as if using that word makes you a reactionary. Yet evil is more manifest than ever. It should be more contained than ever. What happened? Can't we even discuss it??

Since when is a spade a heart?

What have we given up on?

Are we sleeping in or are we in a pew on Easter morning?

Are we who we were meant to be?

RWE?

Right Wing Extremist?

ROE

Where do fish come from that are not fried?

Eggs, dummy.

Egg clusters that make caviar.

It is funny that all fish come from little round gooey things.

Kinda like where we get our beginnings. Mom knows.

Mom raised us all by making sure we did only the right things that she knew.

Well, from her parents' eggs… LOL

The first things we really remember about our Moms are love and rules. She knew life and her role was to protect and nurture.

Our Dads are the same but they have stricter rules… or should have. Boys and girls need to be forged. I worry that the forging process these days is being diluted by political correctness and other shifts in cultures. Social networks tend to be rule-free. Think about it.

"The focus group is ambushing our advantage."

No rules???

When we get engaged there are rules of behavior so the wedding comes off as it should. With both families feeling proud. So the values of the past may have a shot at survival.

Today rules have become political footballs. Fine print infests all rules. So you can't really figure out what a rule is other than from the latest litigation.

There are serious enemies out there. They must be identified and disposed of. Life is not about social networking. There will be no social networking if the current evils are allowed to grow unchecked. Hello?

ROE. Rules Of Engagement have been challenging the soldier for decades. We worry so much about unjust collateral damage that the bad guy is given refuge in our ROE. Bureaucracy is redefining inefficiency and inaction. The special operations warrior has his box rebuilt daily. It is a miracle they don't explode. But they don't. That is who they are.

Get the politicians out of war. Get their fingers off the triggers. The focus group is ambushing our advantage.

Where have all the good rules gone?

Moralities abandoned.

Values lost.

Enemy dis-engaged.

Obvious

Why is the obvious so unobvious to so many?

Why is logic so difficult understand?

Hey, let's go right to Washington for fun. We all postulate out here in the hinterlands that Washington just doesn't get it.

We work hard for a living and to hopefully pay our bills which will allow us to enjoy some things and help a few folk. We like to spend some time with our family and friends, enjoy a meal, and enjoy the sunrise and sunset. Work hard and feel good about yourself. Do good and feel good. Be honest and tell the truth. Then trust can facilitate growth and security. Simple.

We don't need more rules and more of those who regulate them. I thought government was to make our lives more simple and fruitful. And... protect our freedoms. But they seem to be on a Mission Impossible, to make our lives more impossible. What seems obvious to us out here in our towns, businesses, and churches is not on their screens and databases. Is it logical that they don't see our logic? KISS. Keep It Simple Senators.

Is it not obvious that no American can properly fill out their

"Why is the obvious so unobvious to so many?"

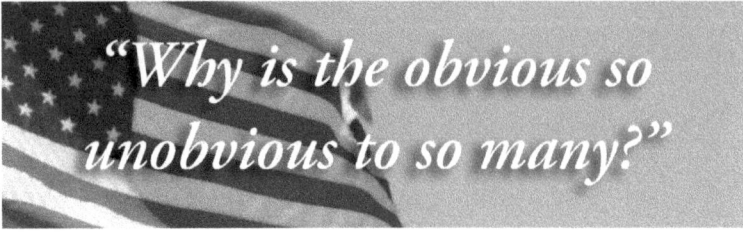

income tax form? Should not the tax system be done away with and replaced with a few flat tax codes? Does IRS stand for Intricate Revenue Stupification? What is the obvious?

Isn't it obvious that speeding is speeding?

Isn't it obvious that debt is debt?

Isn't it obvious that killing is murder?

Isn't it obvious that you go to a doctor if you're sick... not a lawyer?

Isn't it obvious that a family is a family?

Isn't it obvious that a church is for worship?

Isn't it obvious that evil is not good?

Isn't it obvious that common sense is being ignored?

The obvious has become the humor of the bureaucrat. The new obvious is "the essential structuring and parsing of all definitions after vetting by legal."

I am keeping this short as it is obvious that the obvious is not ranking high in the polls and that the upcoming elections will make it moot anyway.

Revolution

1776 again??

Our backs were up against the wall with the rules and laws of the British.

We yearned for freedoms, especially freedom of speech and religion.

Freedoms were being boxed in.

"Common Sense" prevailed.

One thing led to another.

Arms were borne.

Freedom won.

So where is the red line in the sand for freedoms? In the old days there was no information media really. Today we know so much that confusion rules and simplicity is lost. We are losing judgment to the margins of society. The right, the left... now it's the extreme right and the extreme left. All is marginalized. All is demonized. The labeling of labels has created a sea of ignorance and intolerance. Where in the heck are we?

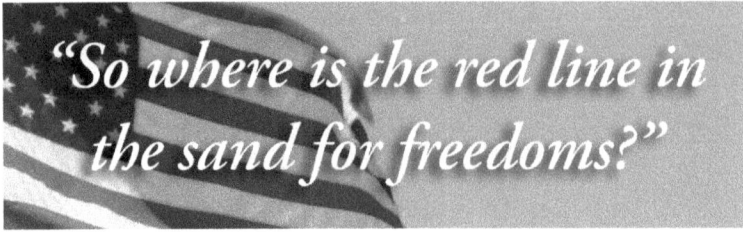

Don't you wish you were back out on some farm somewhere, where nature's brutal indifference is more acceptable? Where hot and cold is preferable to half-truths and denial. Where flooding and wind is preferable to unemployment and uncertainty. Remember the "I can't stand it anymore" guy??

Is there not anyone in Washington who can't stand it anymore?

Reconciliation or revolution are the options. The former is less certain. Let's have a big picnic in front of the Lincoln Memorial and get drunk so when we start shooting at each other we miss. I want a beer and wine revolution, not a social one. Maybe bows and arrows…. Or even better…pumpkin catapults.

Seriously, our nation is in trouble. We have allowed and welcomed the demonization of us, we brothers. My brother has become my labeled enemy. He is tattooed with half-truth.

Forget the unparalleled injustices of the Middle East.

Forget our abominable indifference to international women's rights….

Forget all that.

There is a whiff of real internal revolution in the air.

Streets filled with protesters looming.

Protesters fighting protesters.

Anger and mayhem that only troops, not executive order, can quell.

Which side will take over the country?

This is 2015, not 1776… or is it?

Memorial Day

Our flag flies at half-mast.

Our flag.

The flag of the United States of America.

Our flag allows us to debate, criticize, and protest as much as we want without fear of persecution.

It is amazing how much we love to criticize. Media and social networks are ablaze with condemnation. Oh yes, there are stories of good works.... but those headlines are stolen by scandal and criticism, however intellectually cloaked.

Freedom of speech is the greatest threat to freedom throughout the world. What we take for granted is feared elsewhere. We are under attack by radical this and that because freedom of speech will destroy their power. Terrorism is applied to those willing to speak. Sad.

Graves freshly dug and graves of 1776 abound with sacrifice and tragedy. Tragedy if the life was lost for no reason. Those of us who live have to make those losses have meaning by how we conduct ourselves. The veteran is not that outspoken for he

"The tear in the eye of the Veteran reflects the light of Truth."

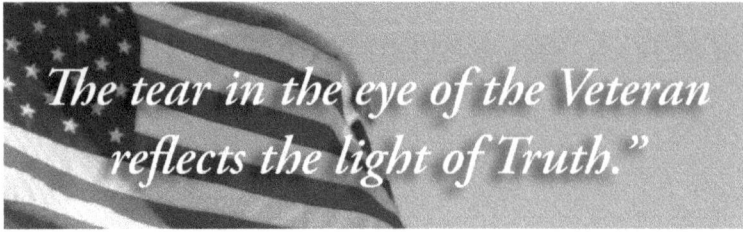

knows the horror of war and the value of freedom. We all too often mock it and abuse it.

It is time we bring dignity and respect back into our lexicon. Yes mam, yes sir. Yes Mother, yes Father.

Our hypocrisy is so much more visible these days. Look at the killings and the excesses of our behavior. Look at pictures of crowds these days and how fat we have become. We mock those who differ. We mock religion. Respect for elders?? Forget it. They are just old people who are not relevant.

On Memorial Day we are bowing our heads to our cell phones and not to those who made this land free.

The tear in the eye of the Veteran reflects the light of Truth.

It knows evil and it knows folly.

Thank you for your service.

27,000 Pages

When I was a kid, things were pretty simple.

If Johnny said something mean to me, I just hit him and that was the end of it.

Then grew up a bit and got my Kentucky driver's license, signed one form, drove the test… and was free for life!

There was a thing called the handshake back then.

It worked for most agreements.

I wasn't old enough for a job or taxes.

Life was easy to understand.

There weren't many lawyers.

I went into the Navy and my income tax form was really simple as pie. You could figure it out. Maybe 2-3 pages, a deduction, and you got a check. This worked for a long time.

I got out and it still was a non-event. Your company supplied your W-2, you deducted your mortgage stuff, some charity, and put a stamp on the envelope. It was a little more for a small business, but the accountant had it figured out.

"There was a thing called the handshake back then."

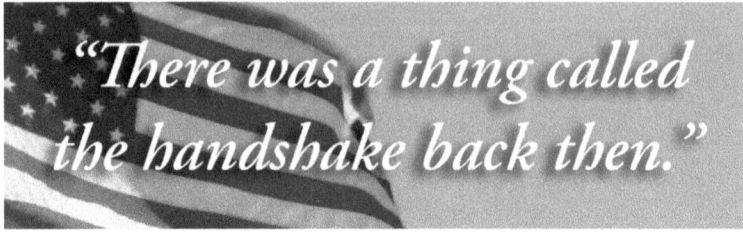

Fast forward. Today's tax code is 27,000 pages.

The fine print tries to outwit the payee. Every possible interpretation is potentially covered in infinite fine print. Hello?? Tilt!! How did this happen? Who is to blame? This is evil.

This is bureaucracy gone wild. Where are the Bureaucracy Police? Where is transparency? It has been stabbed in the aorta by keyboards and fine print. Is this really government protecting us or is it white collar crime on the grandest scale? Where are the environmental watchdogs?

This is our economic environment that is being strangled by an administrative shell game.

Who writes this stuff anyway? Who signs off on it? Isn't it time to say "Throw the bums in jail!"? Every government says they are going to make things simple and they lie to us. Remember the 9-9-9 concept? It may have been brilliant with a few adjustments, but NOT 27,000 pages worth!!!

We need Navy SEAL politicians who will not quit nor flinch in the face of fully armed special interest attorneys. It is time to "just do it". Chuck it all.

And now that we have a concept…. How about applying it to the deficit? The budget. The entitlements. Make a bill a bill with no attachments, no pork, and no special interest addendums. Make everything stand on its own. Just do it.

Well, maybe this postulating is too late.

Maybe 27,000 pages has sealed our fate and the cliff is here.

I see the top of the waterfall 100 yards ahead....

The noise……..aghhh…

See ya.

Hooyah.

War

"War is an ugly thing, but not the ugliest of things. The decayed and degraded state of moral and patriotic feeling which thinks that nothing is worth war is much worse..." (John Stuart Mill).

I just finished an intense book by a Navy SEAL titled "Damn Few". That quote jumped out at me so strong as it is themed throughout all my writings. So let's explore it a little.... And see if we can reject the premise.

As we all know, war is repugnant because of all the innocent people that suffer horribly from wounds and displacement, much less death.

Idiotic regimes, egos, and cultures espouse freedom and compassion for their poor only to subjugate them to false cultures of corruption. While, at the same time, they demonize our liberties and success.

With our great intellects we dismiss their posturing as just illusions of danger. We analyze and yield responsibility to the talking heads and pundits in the media. They are all over perspective, truth, and the infinite postulations of politicians. Are they are more right than we are? We allow them to be.... And

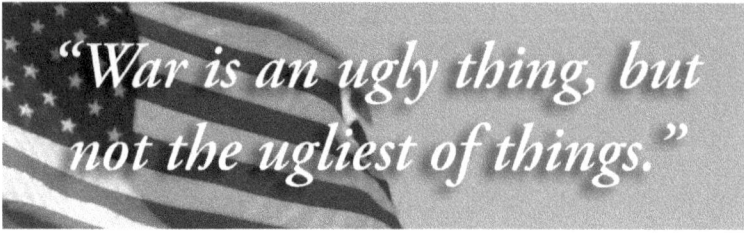

"War is an ugly thing, but not the ugliest of things."

we… become complicit in the advent of war.

I have never seen a body blown to bits or a child with a bullet hole in her head. Do I need to see that to take a stand? Do I need to turn off the TV and do something? Can I stop a bullet coming for some child's brain?

We all have to answer that question. We all have to think about it and take a stand. Not to is to be a coward and an irresponsible adult who chooses to facilitate evil. That's how I call it.

To take a stand means to stand for something.

Where is the line you draw? Does anything have value? Define values. What made this country great? Or when did you think it might have been great?

We are a good people. We are a blessed people. We have a great Constitution and a great history of compassion. Is this worth protection? Do we realize we are on an invisible slippery slope to losing it all? There is a moral decay in our country that is almost systemic. Laws are reducing responsibility.

Behavior is being redefined to permit anything under the umbrella of rights. Sin now has rights. Christians are now being marginalized. Showing the American flag is now problematic.

Labels have proliferated such that anything good is easily categorized as bad. It is so subtle. It is so deadly.

Our internal bickering and blaming is eroding our society. The rest of the world sees it as weakness and the forces of war are being emboldened.

We will be at war again. It may be this year…or next… but it is inevitable the way we are behaving.

"Nothing is worth war" is becoming our motto.

We are actually saying that we will not fight.

We will talk and threaten while our economy and our military erode.

Paper tiger.

Our children aren't worth war?

If you touch my car I will kill you.

Happy

I submit this is the best song ever written. Pharrell Williams. "Can't nothing bring me down….Because I'm happy".

My wife loves the song. Makes me happy. Wanted to share the link. http://www.youtube.com/watch?v=CEN9I8jJ0Nk You really should find a way to view it before you proceed.

All cultures and countries have their set of rules to insure conformity to a vision of achieving happiness for all. Except…. most inevitably fail as they become consumed by the cancers of greed, pride, power, and base evil. Only pretentious facades of happiness and unity are presented in their controlled medias.

But watch this video and sense intuitively the innocence and power of happiness. That joy which we all pursue.

Lies upon lies are presented to citizens as truth. Distorted images of the wrong in our democratic society rather than our amazing outreach of good that is routine.

The USA, the United States Of America, however flawed, promises a better chance of Happy than any other society.

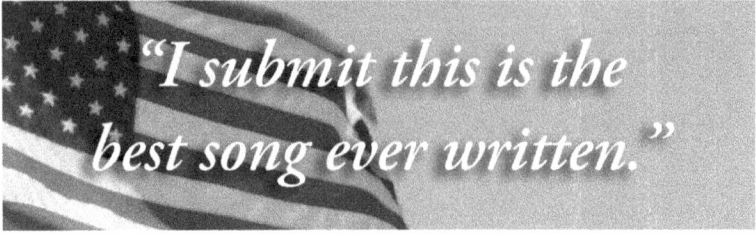

"I submit this is the best song ever written."

Deal with it world.

Too bad.

Get Happy.

Laugh again.

Dance again.

Slide for Life

Water slides are fabulous these days.

They even have them on cruise ships… Go figure.

Kids used to pour water with a hose on the top of a slide in a playground and enjoy the wet ride.

Some big slides got dangerous… but still exciting. Who cares anyway when you are young?

A lot of people want to slide through life. So they throw a little alcohol or drugs on it and push off on the easy downhill ride. Except at the bottom the ladder up has rungs too far apart.

The easy way is always the hardest way. Until you learn that the hardest way is the easiest. We humans try to cut every corner there is. We cut too many moral corners. We try to maneuver around the Truth. Guess where it gets us? Not closer to happiness for sure…

Well, now we are forced to go back to the Nave SEAL O' Course (Obstacle Course) to learn simple lessons. At the Amphibious Base in Little Creek Virginia and also in Coronado California are the only two Slides For life in existence…

There is this 30-40 foot wood frame tower to climb up… At the top is a ladder to climb to then find a way to jump up at the rope that descends across a water pit for maybe 30 yards. But your body has to be on top of the rope to make any time descending. Let's say it is a leap of Faith to get to where you just start. Hey, it snowed too.

BUD/S is all about faith that you won't get killed every time some outrageous task is put forth. Like running up a sand dune backwards…….

Life requires all of us to do the impossible at some point.

Faith is required.

Where do you find Faith?

That is what my 400 chapters in my 1-800 books are all about.

They are damned good.

Look straight forward, never down, and the slide for life can be conquered.

Happy guys at the bottom will greet you.

One World

Celebrities gather and sing "We Are The World"….

Do we?

From space our diversities are irrelevant…

We celebrate our differences and our cultures.

But at birth we do look so alike.

We are family.

When a woman or child is abused anywhere it is really to your family.

Except we can't see it that way.

We desecrate God with intellectual dismissal.

But without Him, there is no family. There is no Father.

The SEALs are some of those who are on the very dangerous front lines of confronting this evil indifference.

To do nothing is like leaving your front door open with your children inside, alone.

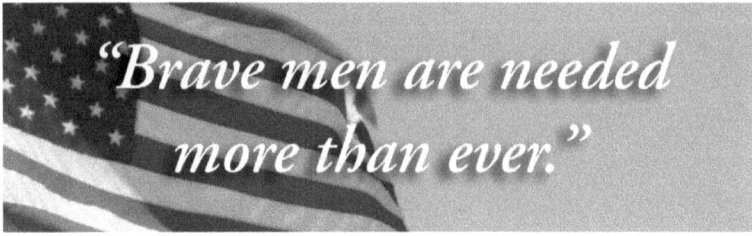

"Brave men are needed more than ever."

There are evil forces out there in nations and religions that wish us harm.

Our heads are in the sand to the cloaked threats of annihilation.

Brave men are needed more than ever.

One world is the noble dream.

"We are the world".

Betelgeuse

Now before you get all excited…

I ask us to put things into perspective.

Whoever becomes President.

"Whoever" (great word, no gender)

Will have to put things in perspective. Our future, our economy, our well-being, and our values need re-alignment. The status quo is not acceptable. The world is more dangerous than ever? Why? We have to dig deep and ask ourselves why. What are we doing that isn't working? What have WE allowed to evolve?

Fine print, regulations, entitlement are some of the few things that are strangling us. Is our declining list of values a factor?

We are searching for a new way to look at things. We want a change in our priorities and especially in our efficiencies.

The "me" has become more important than the "we".

Our new world of instant communications is protecting some but damaging others. Will there be more jealousy or understanding? Can you tweet me your feelings? Don't look up. They say it is a waste of time….

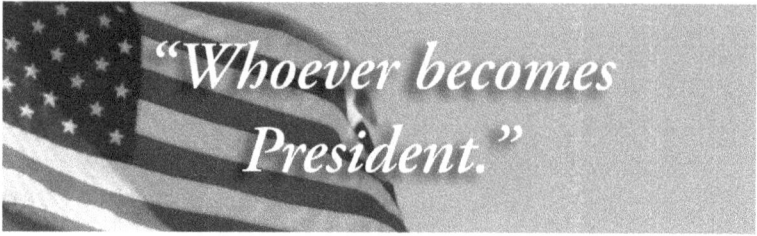

"Whoever becomes President."

"I" am the universe. My universe revolves around "me". Chatters text 24/7.

We have geographical, cultural, economic, race, and political divisions. All being misunderstood by most, and especially by the selfish.

Want a new perspective??

Betelgeuse. I dare you. Go google it. Tweet your observatory.

She is a star in the Orion constellation. She is over 100 million miles in diameter. Maybe much more, but who cares? 590 million light years from us. I bet we look small in that perspective.... Much less the human being....

But within each human being are zillions of entities which change and grow and create. It bleeds, it hopes, it sins, and it loves. Its potential is greater than the numbers of Betelgeuse. Go figure?

So let's get off our political duffs and create a brave new world.

For it will require bravery.

From each of us.

Whoever becomes President.

Debt Dogs

The dogs of war are loose.

Which war?

Middle-East?

Politics?

Financial?

How did we get to the place where there is so much disturbing financial news from so many quarters? We are dithering visions into the ground. Promises abound. Promise Keepers are hard to find.

Government bureaucrats can't keep their promises. The train to Washington derails them from their roots. Special interest money and power makes them cower.

The dogs of debt are howling.

We owe other nations billions and billions. We give billions. We waste billions. There are those who make billions off debt interest. Our credit cards spin money like cotton candy machines.

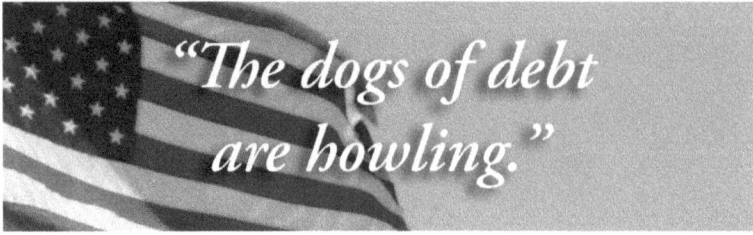

In the good old days you shook hands and owed someone and paid them back.

No fine print.

No attachments to print.

Mailboxes are now avoided.

The incoming mail is liable to be credit card debt.

The dogs of debt are howling.

Trumpster

Back the dumpster up guys…

Over here…

A little more to the Right.

Good. Hold fast.

Some of the political garbage will smell. Just ignore it and fill 'er up.

Political impasse and special interest and greed and laziness and bureaucracy have fattened the corpus politic to a critical mass. Surgery, not diet, is the needed cure. There will be screams and yells and accusations but I am sure Bose can make a new noise cancellation headphone. You need to drown out the naysayer's drums. You will need a donkey filter on the left ear phone and an elephant filter on the right one. Then a special cancellation server to delete the relevant.

It will take a few years to get all the garbage into the Trumpster and truck it away.

That truck will be heavy. It has been special fitted with underside

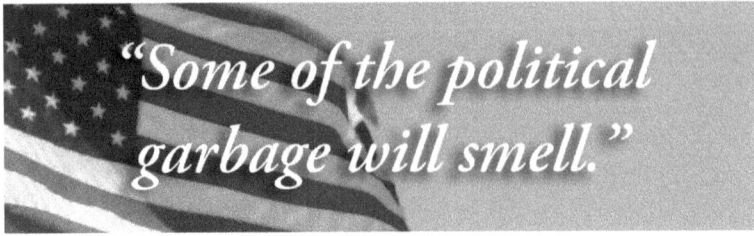

armor to deal with the I.P.D.s. Improvised Political Devices. It's noisy. It has to get the power needed from oil. Solar won't hack it. There will be some exhaust smoke to put up with. But the new fairer winds should send it away.

The contents will be able to fuel the new nuclear peace reactor. One reactor to power the entire planet and the electricity will be free. No more energy wars. All other reactors will be shut down and filled with concrete. Pollutants to air and sea will be cut by half.

I know it's just a dream.

But it's a lot better than what is on the teleprompters.

Bring on the Trumpster.

It's going to the dump.

EPILOGUE

I have been blessed with a journey that has not seen the real poverty or felt the real pain of the majority. Please don't judge me by the immaterial, much less the material. I was born in Bronxville, NY in 1940. Grew up in Louisville and St Louis. Graduated from Yale and went into the Navy. I had the great honor of fulfilling my dream to become a Frogman. I graduated from BUDS Class 31E, Basic Underwater Demolition/Seal School. I was an officer in Underwater Demolition Team 21 which became Seal Team 4 in 1984. I had the honor of recovering several spacecraft, including Gemini 6/7 & AS-201, the very first Apollo Spacecraft to go into space. Wow, did I luck out. Then I spent 40 years in women's retail, in various department stores. Even a year at the World Wrestling Federation... go figure?

I have two great daughters and two grandchildren who have just discovered the water and facemasks. My wife has created probably the #1 women's accessory store in the country as evidenced by how much she is copied. Therein I work and report to her... No comment. LOL.

As you can tell by reading between the lines there is a spiritual side to my journey. Kind of covert as I just want to make a difference unseen.

God Bless You All... Happy Trails.

ACKNOWLEDGEMENTS

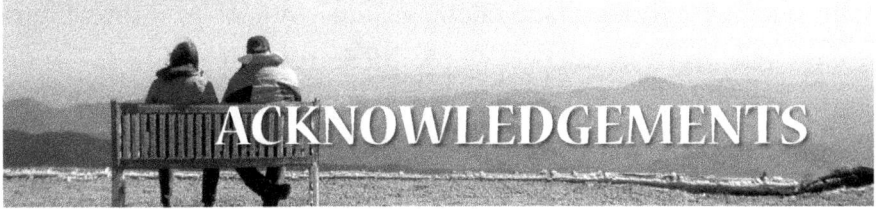

Writing 1-800-OH-MY-DONALD came right out of the blue. I call it the Donald Trump phenomenon. Deep in the heart of America is brooding dissatisfaction with the political establishment. He woke this up. I never thought to write about politics although I already had been.

This book is political commentary and another perspective on the solution to our predicament.

All policies and strategies will fail if we don't find ourselves, our roots. This book is humorous and provocative. Have a ball, I did. And our thanks to the Donald for getting us all up off our asses (political pun).

The chapters average only 300 words. There is no planned order. You can open the book anywhere and read the 2 pages and get a smile and a frown if you catch the serious challenge.

Maybe these books will be found some day and help others make fewer mistakes.

I have to always acknowledge those who make a difference to me. This is the short list.

There are my daughters, Candice and Courtney, who thought they knew their dad, but really didn't. There is my brilliant wife

Christina, who thought she knew her husband. . . . And then there are my friends from the past whose life journeys I do not fully know, and who do not know me now. For in life it is who we become, not who we were.

Then there are the men of my NO Walls Bible Studies and Max Lucado who freed us to think with assurance and humility. Leading me to new friendships of the Highest quality.

Lastly, there are Sandra Simmons-Dawson and Brian Dawson who helped edit and format the books, website, and marketing. Their firm, Money Management Solutions, Inc. dba Customer Finder Marketing http://customerfindermarketing.com/ is a gem.

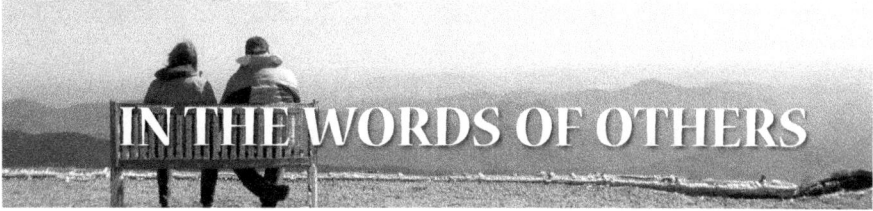

IN THE WORDS OF OTHERS

Reviews for 1-800-I-Am-Unhappy
(Volumes 1 and 2)

"This is a book by a man of many directions and passions. Straightforward yet thought provoking. Loyal to his convictions and country. And brave. Sharing. Warrior. Humanitarian."

Jeff Lytle, Editorial Page Editor, Naples Daily News

"As a friend, Chris has helped me understand the inherent conflicts embedded in the language of 'political correctness' and how it attempts, and frequently succeeds, in disguising and defeating the 'truth.' Chris is engaged in a rhetori- cal battle — we need his insight."

William Lord, a 32-year-veteran Executive Producer and Vice-President of ABC News, and Professor of Journalism at Boston University

"Chris writes like he lives. As a man of distinction, he is a voice for the poor, a champion of the truth and a friend of strong character and conviction. His word and his service are a blessing to all who encounter him."

Vann R. Ellison, President/CEO, St. Matthew's House, Inc.

"My nickname for Chris is "Dream-Catcher"- because that's who he is to me. He is my mentor in how to give on His behalf. Freely and generously, Chris offers both words, "God bless you!", and gifts. And all the while he is making a compelling and powerful statement. Chris Bent has discovered a beautiful way to live!"

Rev. Dr. Ruth Merriam, The Church on the Cape (U.M.C.), Cape Porpoise, Maine

"Chris Bent is a very unusual person – Navy SEAL, Yale graduate, successful business owner, and radical Christian who is comfortable talking with anyone at any level in society. He doesn't just talk about faith or caring about the poor, Chris actually lives his faith and he works with the poor. His smile is genuine and reflects his deep joy in life, America, hard work, people and (most definitely) God. I have enjoyed reading his writings; they are different, often hard hitting and sometimes maybe even a little wild. Each one gives a fresh perspective on contemporary lives, reflecting Chris' intel- ligence and faith. Chris enjoys moving mountains."

Rev. Dr. Ted Sauter, Senior Pastor, North Naples United Methodist Church

Reviews for 1-800-For-Women-Only

"It is amazing that a man would want to write about women. That is a change, but Chris has a sense of humor that can make you laugh. Women will enjoy this book and men may gain new insight."

Dorothy K. Ederer, O.P., Director of Campus Ministry,
St. John Student Center, East Lansing, Michigan

"Light, refreshing take on some not so light topics. Wrapped in silliness and wit are serious, social and moral truths that challenge us to be more than ordinary."

Peggy Ryba, Membership Director, North Naples Church, Naples, Florida

"Chris is like a modern day prophet, throwing modern day concepts and concerns out there for us to contemplate. The seeds he tosses can land on sand or soil depending on the reader. I suggest you pull up a nice spot in your garden and sit down and read…then allow some of his thoughts to germinate in your life! "

Mia Guinan, Owner, Gourmet Gang, Camp Trident, Virginia Beach VA

"Paradox is a person that combines contradictory features. Chris Bent is a paradox. Reading his most recent works I am not surprised by the depth, humor, passion and spirituality. In spite of mixed content the flow between chapters allows you to enjoy the paradox. Chris' muses have caused a few smiles; some ponderings and touched my heart. Let this Paradox of a Man walk up to you and continue the conversation.
Nancy Lascheid, RN, BSN, Co-Founder, Neighborhood Health Clinic, Naples, Florida

"1-800-For-Women-Only or the "Mystery of Women" is interesting because it is brutally accurate. In fact, it is frightening to read the explanations of characteristics of women. Many of these things I had not even been aware of, but they are "right on target". The book is written with great sensitivity and insight. I never got the feeling that women were criticized, but accepted as observed. It is an easy fun read and a great gift to give to a friend or even a son who is even thinking of getting married. As the mother of three sons, I know it is true; "Heartfelt is at the core of being. Being somebody."
Sue Lester, Volunteer, Children's Coalition of
Collier County, Pilot Club, Naples, Florida

"Chris Bent's extraordinary life has given him a perspective that so very few have. His insight comes not only from his incredible experiences but from his deeply rooted sense of responsibility, caring, and love for others. His thoughtful mind is not on idle, but instead always on overdrive, crystallizing in well thought out words those concepts that would have many times escaped us, were it not for the efforts of this author to engage, care deeply, and then, as Chris has done so remarkably here, write."
Jennifer L. Whitelaw, Attorney, Whitelaw Legal Group, Naples, FL

Reviews for 1-800-Laughing-Out-Loud

"Chis is a stew: meat, potatoes, veggies, gravy, biscuits and mustard. A warm, tender mix of good taste, generous servings, and something for all appetites! Chris mixes a Hunter S. Thompson "Gonzo Journalism" writing style with a Soupy Sales "Pie in the Face" sense of humor. Chris writes about: Life Values, Family, Self, Respect, Good & Evil. His perspective of life's Value Proposition engages our brain to think about ourselves and others. Chris' previous books are from the Heart and Soul. Take his counsel of his life's experience. There is good advice in each chapter! You will enjoy each word like every bite of a good stew."

Gerry Ross, Executive, Pratt & Whitney (Retired)

"Chris Bent is the type of guy you want to share a cold beer with at the end of a lousy day and have him philosophize on the real meaning of life. Since you might not have that opportunity anytime soon let me suggest you read 1-800-LAUGHING-OUT-LOUD. Perfect title for the book, because when reading it you will."

Nancy Lascheid, RN, BSN, Co-Founder, Neighborhood Health Clinic, Naples, Florida

Reviews for 1-800-Oh-My-Goodness

"With 1-800-Oh-My-Goodness, Chris Bent offers his thoughts on a variety of topics, in order to amuse, inspire, and challenge any reader. With his witty insight, and perspective forged from life experience, Chris seeks to help us all become better individuals."

Michael Hopkins, Attorney, Naples, FL

"In this book Chis is honest and open with the reader. He definitely gives you a lot to ponder. You can't wait to see what he is going to share next."

Dorothy K. Ederer O.P., Director of Campus Ministry, St. John Student Center

"Oh my goodness", Chris has again presented a faith filled and thought provoking book. His stream of thought, that often reads more like poetry than prose, will cause you to rethink moments of life in a context of love and promise."

Rev Jean Moorman Brindel, CFRE, AFP, Associate Director of Development, Emeritus United Theological Seminary, Dayton Ohio

"Honest, incisive, poetic and profound: the writings of Chris Bent. Passion for people, the nation and the world spring from his pages; provocative questions leap from the shortest chapters ever. Silent voices speak in these pages and nothing is to be taken for granted, for life and love run deep between the lines of 1-800- Oh-My-Goodness. "

Wendy J. Deichmann, PhD, President, United Theological Seminary

Reviews for 1-800-For-SEALS-Only

"Pungent, cogent, wistful, idealistic, naive, wise, — all in no particular sequence, reflecting a view of life that it is all unpredictable, and it is mental, physical & moral preparation that will sustain us… there are life lessons and observations here for anyone and everyone…."

Lt (jg) James Hawes, BUDS 29E, SEAL, CIA, (He was the First SEAL In Africa)…(sadly was my UDTR Instructor too)

"Who knew SEALs could write? (LOL) But what Chris does with his gift is really less "writing" than it is expressing the "unwritten." We all have our thoughts; and Frogmen have certain very special and unique shared experiences. Chris puts the pen to the task of relating what we (the Frogs) have experienced and what we (all of his readers) now observe in sharing the experience of the world around us. It's challenging and funny (if you've been through a "real Hell Week"), and sometimes sad. But hey, isn't life? Hooyah!"

Timothy Phillips, SEAL, BUDS 166, ST-8, ST-4

| www.ChrisBent.com

"Chris - great stuff…as always. "Hooyah Mike"…"Every sin is a grenade"…"My wife is my swim buddy"…great thoughts as only a SEAL can put into words. I love it and will BUY a few copies for my Assistant Sergeant at Arms to read to guide their young lives… Hooyah Chris and see you soon!"

Phil King, Sergeant at Arms, NC Senate, BUDS 32

"Mr. Bent's words of wisdom on some of the evolutions of U. S. Navy SEAL training are demonstrated to apply to everyday life with such simplicity. God, Family, Country, is the essence of being an honorable and patriotic American. It is the ethos of the Navy SEAL credo. The band of brothers whose lives are bonded as one in being; all for one and one for all! Nothing in this world feels better to receive in life as the emblem, the SEAL Trident, of a true warrior and to receive into one's heart the holy trinity! Hooyah! The only easy day was yesterday!"

Erasmo Elijah Riojas (Doc Rio) HMC (SEAL) Ret.

"I am a SEAL Teammate of LT. Chris Bent. During our years of serving our country as Naval Special Warfare Operatives, Chris always manifested that "Can Do" attitude so necessary for success in what many would consider: "A tough way to make a living!"

Among other sub-specialties, Chris and I had the honor of being the Platoon Commanders who would "Recover Astronauts!" Within the pages of "1-800-FOR-SEALS-ONLY", you will get to see the mind-set of students going through BUDS Training (still the toughest Military Training in the World) with most Classes experiencing an over 80% Drop Out Rate! Chris masterfully combines our training to current issues existing today. A Giant HOOYAH for a must read publication! 1-800-FOR-SEALS-ONLY is awarded a big BRAVO ZULU from your old Teammates!"

Dr. Frank Cleary, OIC, Seventh Platoon, ST-2 (Ret.)

"One need only look into the night sky to recognize that there is brilliance in chaos. One need only read this book to realize the same. Intertwined in stories, random thoughts, and opinions one will find extraordinary pearls of wisdom in here………..and a lot of them. Chris is brilliant."

Navy SEAL Commander

"Dear Frogfather, Your writings remind me of the lessons and examples that were taught to me and my siblings by my parents, grandparents and the nuns that taught me in parochial school. I am so blessed to have them in my life. We are also blessed to have you because you have taken the time and effort to put down in writing your thoughts. They are insightful, and positive, to help us lead a better life. Thank you."

Maureen Murphy, Mother of LT. Michael Murphy,
Medal of Honor recipient, BUD/S Class 236, SDVT-1

"Five Stars for the FROGFATHER! This is a great book, and should be required reading…."

Commander (SEAL) Tom Hawkins, USN, Ret., author, NSW Historian

"Chris Bent has again taken his many and varied life experiences and applied them to life in general and "how to do it right". This book is clearly for everyone, not just SEAL's. Life was never meant to be easy and all of us can take away something from this book and the Frogman saying "The only easy day was yesterday". Even if it is the hard way….do the right thing.

From one Frogman to another I say to Chris, your eulogy (chapter 75) should be read when the time comes: Teammate, seen or unseen, you truly have made a difference!

Hooyah 1-800-For-SEALS-Only!"

Mike Macready, SEAL Team One, BUD/S 49 West Coast

"Chris Bent's latest 1-800 offering certainly gets my SEAL of approval... Using his own unique blend of insight, intellect and inspiration, Chris lifts parallels from the rich history and tradition behind the US Navy SEALs to provide challenging questions and equally thought provoking answers to this experience that we call life. In this social-networking, politically-corrected day and age where common sense, discipline and values seem to have fallen by the wayside, Chris Bent cuts through like a K-Bar to remind us all exactly what is of the utmost importance."

Darren A. Greenwell - NSW Historian, Researcher, Collector

www.ingramcontent.com/pod-product-compliance
Lightning Source LLC
Chambersburg PA
CBHW071523040426
42452CB00008B/867